文史哲英譯叢刊 6

原野之聲
Voice of the Wilderness

林明理 著（Author：Dr. Lin Ming-Li）
非馬 譯（Translator：Dr. William Marr）

文史哲出版社印行

國家圖書館出版品預行編目資料

原野之聲 / 林明理著；非馬譯. -- 初
版--臺北市：文史哲，民 108.01
　　頁；公分（文史哲英譯叢刊；6）
中英對照
ISBN 978-986-314-453-3（平裝）

851.486　　　　　　　　108001894

文史哲英譯叢刊　　6

原　野　之　聲

著　　者：林　　　明　　　理
譯　　者：非　　　　　　　馬
出版者：文　史　哲　出　版　社
http://www.lapen.com.tw
e-mail：lapen@ms74.hinet.net
登記證字號：行政院新聞局版臺業字五三三七號
發 行 人：彭　　　正　　　雄
發 行 所：文　史　哲　出　版　社
印 刷 者：文　史　哲　出　版　社
臺北市羅斯福路一段七十二巷四號
郵政劃撥帳號：一六一八〇一七五
電話 886-2-23511028・傳真 886-2-23965656

定價新臺幣五〇〇元 彩色版一二六〇元

二〇一九年（民國一〇八）一月初版

原 野 之 聲

目 次　contents

二、已刊登的詩作（尚未翻譯區）
Published poems (not yet translated)

六、附錄 appendix

藝術家

在這天空解構
大地顛覆的
虛擬後現代
居然还用
那傳統得不能再傳統
寫實得不能再寫實的手法
漫山遍野潑撒
原色的紅与黃
成为一幅幅
明亮匀稱和諧完整且充滿诗意的
現代畫面
再一次讓你们
張口結舌

非馬
于芝加哥 2018年 11月 27日

非馬祝賀林明理詩人出版「原野之聲」寄來的手稿

THE ARTIST

in this postmodern time
of deconstructed sky and earth
she still employs the traditional technique
pouring red and yellow
over mountains and plains
to become a modern painting of autumn
brilliant, harmonious and full of meaning
astonishing us
one more time

William Marr

2018.11.28, Chicago

林明理（Dr. Lin Ming-Li）簡介

　　林明理，1961 年生，臺灣雲林縣人，中國文化大學大陸問題研究所法學碩士，美國世界文化藝術學院榮譽文學博士（2013.10.21 頒授）。曾任屏東師範學院講師，現任臺灣「中國文藝協會」理事、中華民國新詩學會理事，北京「國際漢語詩歌協會」理事，詩人評論家。2013.5.4 獲第 54 屆「中國文藝獎章」文學類「詩歌創作獎」。2012.9.9.人間衛視『知道』節目專訪林明理 1 小時，播出於第 110 集「以詩與畫追夢的心─林明理」。台灣「文化部」贊助，民視『飛越文學地景』拍攝林明理四首詩作錄影（淡水紅毛城之歌）（2018.11.03 民視新聞首播）、（白冷圳之戀）（2017.7.15 民視新聞首播）、（歌飛阿里山森林）（2016.12.24 民視新聞首播）、〈寫給蘭嶼之歌〉（2016.11.19 民視新聞首播）、（淡水紅毛城之歌）（2018.11.03 民視新聞首播）。

　　著有《秋收的黃昏》、《夜櫻--詩畫集》、《新詩的意象與內涵--當代詩家作品賞析》、《藝術與自然的融合--當代詩文評論集》、《湧動著一泓清泉─現代詩文評論》、《用詩藝開拓美─林明理談詩》、《林明理報刊評論》、《行走中的歌者─林明理談詩》、《海頌─林明理詩文集》、《林明理散文集》、《名家現代詩賞析》、《現代詩賞析》。以及詩集《山楂樹》、《回憶的沙漏》（中英對照）、《清雨塘》、（中英對照）、《山居歲月》（中英對照）、《夏之吟》（中英法對照）、《默喚》（中英法對照）、《我的歌》（中法對照）、《諦聽》（中英對照）、《原野之聲》（中英對照）。她的詩畫被收錄編於山西大學新詩研究所 2015 年編著 《當代著名漢語詩人詩書畫檔案》、詩作六首被收錄於《雲林縣青少年臺灣文學讀本》，評論作品被碩士生研究引用數十篇論文，作品包括詩畫、散文與評論散見於海內外學刊及詩刊、報紙等。中國學報刊物包括有《南京師範大學文學院學報》、《青島師範學院學報》、《鹽城師範學報》等三十多篇，臺灣的國圖刊物《全國新書資訊月刊》二十六篇，還有在中國大陸的詩刊報紙多達五十種刊物發表，如《天津文學》、《安徽文學》、《香港文學》等。在臺灣《人間福報》已發表上百篇作品，在《臺灣時報》、《笠詩刊》與《秋水詩刊》等刊物也常發表作品，另外，在美國的刊物《世界的詩》或報紙《亞特蘭大新聞》等也有發表作品。總計發表的創作與評論作品已達千篇以上。

Dr. Lin Ming-Li was born in 1961 in Yunlin, Taiwan. She holds a Master's Degree in Law and lectured at Pingtung Normal College. A poetry critic, she is currently serving as a director of the Chinese Literature and Art Association, the Chinese New Poetry Society, and Beijing's International Association of Chinese Poetry. On the 4th of May, 2013, she won the Creative Poetry Prize in the 54th Chinese Literature and Arts Awards. On the 21st of October 2013, she received a Doctor of Literature degree from America's World Culture and Art Institute. On the 9th of September 2012, the World Satellite TV Station in Taiwan broadcast her interview, "Lin Ming-Li: The Heart that Pursues a Dream with Poetry and Painting". FTV (FORMOSA TELEVISION) videoed four poems by her, namely, "Fortress San Domingo, Song of Danshui" (2018.11.03 premiere). "Love of the Bethlehem Ditch" (2017.07.15 premiere). "Songs Fill the Forest of Mt. Ali" (2016.12.24 premiere) and "Ode to the Orchid Island" (2016.11.19 premiere).

Her publications include *An Autumn Harvest Evening, Night Sakura: Collection of Poems and Paintings, Images and Connotations of New Poetry : Reading and Analysis of the Works of Contemporary Poets, The Fusing of Art and Nature: Criticism of Contemporary Poetry and Literature, The Gushing of a Pure Spring: Modern Poetry Criticism, Developing Beauty with Poetic Art: Lin Ming-Li On Poetry, A Collection of Criticism from Newspapers and Magazines, The Walking Singer: Lin Ming-Li On Poetry, Ode to the Sea: A Collection of Poems and Essays of Lin Ming-Li,* Appreciation of the Work of Famous Modern Poets, Appreciation of the work of Modern Poets and *Lin Ming-Li's Collected Essays.*

Her poems were anthologized in *Hawthorn Tree, Memory's Hourglass,* (Chinese/English), *Clear Rain Pond* (Chinese/English), *Days in the Mountains* (Chinese/English), *Summer Songs* (Chinese/English/French) , *Silent Call* (Chinese/English/French) and *My song* (Chinese/French) ,Listen (Chinese/English) , Voice of the Wilderness(Chinese/English).

Many of her poems and paintings are collected in *A Collection of Poetry, Calligraphy and Painting by Contemporary Famous Chinese Poets,* compiled in 2015 by New Poetry Research Institute of Shanxi University. Six of her poems are included in *Taiwanese Literary Textbook for the Youth of Yunlin County.* Her review articles have been quoted in theses by many graduate students. Over a thousand of her works, including poems, paintings, essays, and criticisms have appeared in many newspapers and academic journals at home and abroad.

林明理博士畫作及照片刊登區

Dr. Lin Ming-Li's paintings and photo publication area

林明理老師和涂文權
導演合照。

照片 1-3.2015.06.25，
- 林明理老師應邀於民
視「飛閱文學地景」
節目製作於台北市
「齊東詩舍」錄影及
訪談，三張合照刊登在
美國《亞特蘭大新聞》
Atlanta Chinese News，
2018/06/29。

Photo 1-3.2018.06.25, Dr. Lin Ming-Li was invited to the FTV
program video and interviews, with the production team and the
director's three photos, published in the US "Atlanta Chinese
News", 2018/06/29.

照4.民視 FTV「飛閱文學地景」執行製作石宛蓉拍攝林明理老師手寫錄影的詩作「淡水紅毛城之歌」，2018/06/25 下午於齊東詩舍。

2018.06.25
齊東詩社
民視 飛閱文學地景
金系列
林明理詩作 淡水紅毛城

照5.林明理詩人錄影後手寫的詩作，2018/06/25。

照6. 2018/02/02 刊登美國《亞特蘭大新聞》報導林明理博士出版第19本新書《諦聽 LISTEN》的書訊，及義大利《國際詩新聞 IPN》

INTERNATIONAL POETRY NEWS報導，由義大利詩人及主編 Giovanni G. Campisi寫的書訊《諦聽 LISTEN》一則。

照 7. 刊美國《亞特蘭大新聞》，2018/06/15。

照 8

獲獎照 9.

PRO Winners

2018 年 10 月 22 日，下午 3:16
　　Time to announce our **WBP Winners** from last week's **Featured Collections selected by our editors from our BTP Pro Pages.**
Another great collection of some of the most outstanding photography by amazing photographers!
Thanks to our amazing team for all their hard work. Please be sure to update your tags.
Interested in having a chance to be here?
Please read and be sure to use to correct tags so we do not miss your work. bit.ly/proproject (Pro Pages Team) *Our beautiful cover photo comes from: +Sergey StratovCongratulations go to: +博士林明理
https://plus.google.com/collection/sWVbeE　Pro Winners WBP Oct 14-20 2018

照 10. .刊美國《亞特蘭大新聞》，2018/10/19 →

←照 11. .刊美國《亞特蘭大新聞》，
2018/10/19.

↑ 照 12.刊美國《亞特蘭大新聞》，2018/10/26。

↑ 獲獎照 13.林明理攝影作品
(red lotus
and damselfly)

照 13

BTP Flower Pro
BTP PRO FLOWER FEATURED COLLECTION
2018 年 10 月 23 日, 上午 2:21
+博士林明理 It's my pleasure to add your excellent photo to our **PRO
FLOWER FEATURED COLLECTION** Be sure to follow our wonderful
collections to see many great photos including yours.
Have a wonderful day!
(Heinfried Küthe)

譯詩刊登的畫作

圖 1.
一刊台灣《人間福報》 The Merit Times，
2018/01/25。
一 刊 義 大 利 《 國 際 詩 新 聞 IPN 》
INTERNATIONAL POETRY NEWS，
2018/01/14，中文及義大利語。

圖 2
一 刊 臺 灣 《 臺 灣 時 報 》 Taiwan
Times，2017/12/27。

圖 3 ─刊美國《亞特蘭大新聞》，
2018.02.02，中英法及西班牙語譯，
圖文。

圖 5. 刊美國《亞特蘭大
新聞》，2018/02/09。

圖 4. 刊美國《亞特蘭大新聞》，
2018/01/26。

圖 7. 刊美國《亞特蘭大
新聞》，2018/02/09。

圖 6. 刊美國《亞特蘭大新聞》，
2018/02/09。

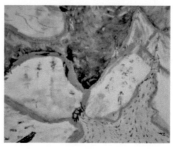

圖 6. 刊美國《亞特蘭大
新聞》，2018/02/16。

圖 9. 刊美國《亞特蘭大新聞》，
2018/02/16。

圖 10. 刊美國《亞特蘭大
新聞》，2018/02/16。

圖 12. 刊美國《亞特蘭大新聞》，
2018/02/23。

圖 11. 刊美國《亞特蘭大
新聞》，2018/02/16。

圖 14. 刊美國《亞特蘭大新聞》，
2018/03/02。

圖 13
刊美國
《亞特
蘭大新
聞》，
2018/
06/8。

圖 15
刊美國《
亞特蘭大
新聞》，
2018/03/
02

.圖 16　刊美國《亞特蘭大新聞》，
　　　　2018/03/09。

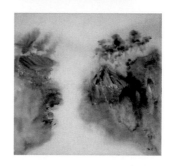

.圖 17　刊美國《亞特蘭大新聞》，
　　　　2018/03/09。

圖 18　刊美國《亞特蘭大新聞》，
　　　　2018/03/09。

圖 19　刊美國《亞特蘭大新聞》，
　　　　2018/03/16。

圖 20　刊美國《亞特蘭大新聞》，2018/03/09。

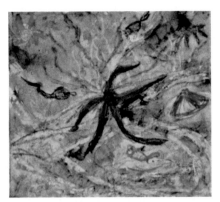

圖 21. 刊美國《亞特蘭大新聞》，
　　　 2018/03/16。

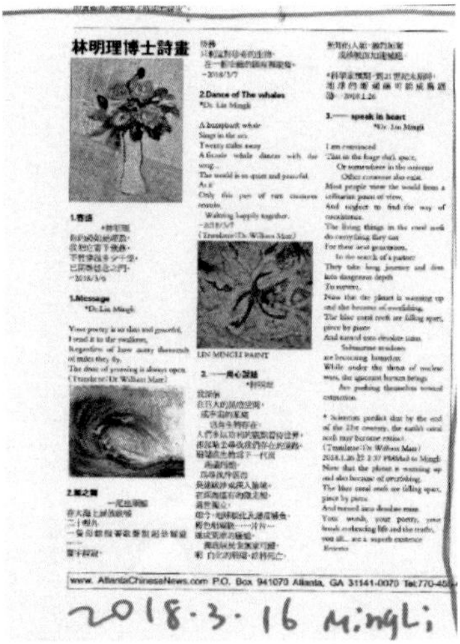

圖 22. 刊美國《亞特蘭大新
　　　 聞》，2018/03/16。

圖 23. 刊臺灣《臺灣時報》，台灣
　　　 文學版，2018/03/14

圖 24

圖 25.　刊美國《亞特蘭大新聞》，
　　　　2018/03/30。

圖 26.   圖 27 刊《臺灣時報》   圖 29

圖 28 刊《臺灣時報》，2018/07/04。

圖 29-1

刊美國《亞特
蘭大新聞》：
圖 26　2018/03/30。
圖 27　2018/07/04。
圖 29　2018/07/06。
圖 30　2018/04/13。
圖 31　2018/04/13。

圖 30

圖 31

攝影/圖 32. -刊美國《亞特蘭
大新聞》，2018/04/13。

圖 33.刊臺灣《臺灣時報》，
2018/04/11。

圖 34. 刊臺灣《臺灣時報》，
2018/04/25。

圖 35. 刊美國《亞特蘭大
新聞》，2018/05/04

圖 36. 刊美國《亞特蘭大新
聞》，2018/05/11，－刊臺灣
《臺灣時報》，2018/09/26。

圖 37. 刊臺灣《臺灣時報》，
台灣文學版，2018/05/17

圖 38.刊亞特蘭大新聞，
2018.05.25

圖 39.刊亞特蘭大新聞，
2018.05.25

圖 40.刊臺灣時報，
2018.05.23

圖 41.刊臺灣時報，
2018.07.18

圖 42.刊臺灣時報，
2018.06.06

圖 43.刊華文現代詩，．
第 18，2018.08

圖 44. 刊美國《亞特蘭大新聞》，
2018/06/08，刊臺灣《臺灣時
報》台灣文學版，2018/06/13。

圖 45. 刊臺灣《臺灣時報》
2018/07/13。

圖 45.-1 刊《人間福報》，2018/07/12。

圖 45.-1 刊《人間福報》，2018/07/12。

圖 45-2 刊美國《亞特蘭大
新聞》2018/08/03 及
2018/08/17。

圖 45-3.-刊臺灣《臺灣時報》，2018/07/13，圖文。
圖 45-4.-刊美國《亞特蘭大新聞》2018/08/03，圖文。

圖 46. 刊美國《亞特蘭大新
聞》2018/06/29，圖文。

圖 47. 林明理/油畫 刊臺灣
《人間福報》刊《臺灣時報》

圖 48. 林明理/油畫　刊《臺
灣時報》，2018/09/05，亞特
蘭大新聞，2018/09/28。

圖 49.刊《人間福報》，2018/
10/04，美國《亞特蘭大新聞》，
2018/10/19，2018/10/12。

圖 50 刊臺灣時報，2018.12.19。

未譯詩刊登的畫作：

圖 1.刊在美國《Atlanta Chinese News》，2018/01/12。

圖 2.刊美國《亞特蘭大新聞》，2018/01/05。刊臺灣《臺灣時報》

圖 3.刊美國《亞特蘭大新聞》，2017/12/22.

圖 5. 刊美國《亞特蘭大新聞》，2017/12/29，刊臺灣《臺灣時報》，台灣文學版，2018/08/01。

圖 5.

圖 7. 刊美
國《亞特蘭
大新聞》
2018.01.05
圖文。

圖 6. 刊美國《亞特蘭大新聞》，
2018/01/05。

圖 13.刊《臺灣時報》，2018/10/03
美國《亞特蘭大新聞》，2018/10/12。

圖 8.

圖 8.刊《亞特蘭大新
聞》，2018/08/10，
刊《臺灣時報》，
2018 /08/29。

圖 10.刊《亞特蘭大新
聞》，2018/07/20，
刊《臺灣時報》，
2018/10/19。

圖 10.

圖 15.刊臺灣《臺灣時報》，
2018/10/31。

圖 15.林明理攝影作品
刊美國《亞特蘭大
新聞》，2018/11/02。

圖 4.詩作獲 2018 年 1 月 4 日浙江省麗水市「秀山麗水，詩韻處
州」地名詩歌大賽三等獎，臺灣林明理詩（寫給麗水的歌）。

一、中英譯詩刊登區

English poetry

1. 如果我是隻天堂鳥

如果我是隻天堂鳥
　　我將永不忘記
回到故鄉
回到雨林這天堂領域。
所有生靈的樂趣
　　在沼澤和雲霧間
我飛上了
　　　一樹高枝
獨自舞著，忘情的跳躍
還能遠遠地望得見
部落，從黃昏
　　到森林的盡頭。

Lin Mingli/painting

*2018.1.5 觀賞 BBC Earth 影片介紹天堂鳥（bird-of-paradise），有感而作。牠是巴布亞紐幾內亞 Papua New Guinea 的國鳥。

－2018.1.7

1.　If I am a bird of paradise

*Dr.Lin Ming-Li

If I am a bird of paradise
　　I will never forget
To return home
Return to the rainforest paradise.
All creatures have fun
　　Between the swamps and clouds
I fly atop
　　The branches of a tall tree
Dance alone, jumping up and down
I can also see the tribe in the distance
From dusk
　　To the end of the forest.

＊　2018.1.5　Watched　a　BBC　Earth　video　introducing　the
Bird-of-paradise, a national bird of Papua New Guinea.
－2017.1.13
（Translator：Dr.William Marr　非馬　英譯）

義大利語譯

1.   *Se fossi un uccello del paradiso*

Non dimenticherei mai
Di tornare a casa
Tornerei nel paradiso della foresta pluviale
Dove tutte le creature si divertono
Tra le paludi e le nuvole
Volerei dentro
I rami di un grande albero
Danzerei da solo, dimenticherei di saltare
Potrei ancora vedere lontano
Le tribù, al tramonto
Alla fine della foresta.

Uccello Paradiso
della Papua Nuova Guinea
Dipinto e poesia di Lin Ming-Li
Traduzione in italiano di
Giovanni G. Campisi

2018.1.18　今天 於 6:11 AM
Hi Ming-Li,

Ho tradotto e pubblicato la tua poesia "Bird Paradise".
Dimmi se ti piace.
Un abbraccio.
Giovanni
　　－刊臺灣《人間福報》，2018.1.25 圖文。
　　－刊義大利《國際詩新聞 IPN》，2018.1.14
　　　圖文，中文及義大利語。

Athanase Vantchev de Thracy 於 2018/1/25 (週四) 9:52 PM Mail 寫道：

Dear Mingli,

I send you the translation of your beautiful poem :

法文語譯

1. SI JE SUIS UN OISEAU DE PARADIS

Je suis un oiseau de paradis,
　　Je n'oublierai jamais
De rentrer à la maison,
De retourner au paradis de la forêt tropicale.
Toutes les créatures s'amusent, toutes,
　　Celles des marais et celles des nuages !
Je me pose au sommet
　　D'un grand arbre,
Je danse seul dans ses vertes branches
Sautant du haut en bas,
Je peux aussi voir au loin les tribus
Évoluant dans le crépuscule
　　Tout au bout de la forêt.

（Traduit en français par Athanase Vantchev de Thracy）

－英譯刊美國（Poems of the world）
季刊，2016 冬季號，頁 9.
－中英譯刊美國（亞特蘭大新聞），
2017.1.20.圖文

INTERNATIONAL POETRY

NEWS

NAUSIKA ASVESTA VINCITRICE
DEL CONCORSO "POETA DELL'ANNO 2017"

NAUSIKA ASVESTA

1^ posto	Nausika Asvesta	Rodi	Grecia	Bignita
2^ posto	Arlün Casotti	Genova	Italia	I doni dei Signore
ex equo	Miltiadis Dovas	Perama	Grecia	Cielo limpido
3^ posto	Teresinka Pereira	Toledo	U.S.A.	Fidel Castro
ex-equo	Panagiota Tsertekidou	Katerini	Grecia	Numero 4
4^ posto	Egisto Salvi	Fano	Italia	Per te
ex-equo	M. Isabel Guerra Garcia	Santa Maria	Spagna	Libertà zittita
5^ posto	Maria Archondi Vigli	Pireo	Grecia	Nella nostra città
ex equo	Sara Ciampi	Genova	Italia	2 giugno, festa della Repubblica
6^ posto	Hilda Augusta Schiavoni	Irriville	Argentina	Sogni polverizzati
ex-equo	Georgios Skamnakis	Molai	Grecia	Corpo di sirone le tue lettere
7^ posto	Susanna Pagano	Forli	Italia	Vorrei
ex-equo	Melita Toka Karakaliou	Salonicco	Grecia	Lo zero
8^ posto	Chicha Cereceido Rego	La Puebla	Spagna	La volpe e il somaro
ex-equo	Aristotelis Tsakonas	Korydallos	Grecia	Verità
9^ posto	Maurizio Collitani	Prato	Italia	La Milano Sanremo del centenario
ex-equo	Potis Katrakis	Pireo	Grecia	Gioia e dolore
10^ posto	M. Consuelo Pons Liriente	Mosroles	Spagna	L'amicizia

Per partecipare al prossimo concorso letterario "Gran Premio d'Autore", si prega di contattare la segreteria per richiedere il bando e altre informazioni utili all'indirizzo: Edizioni Universum | Via Italia 6 | 98070 Capri Leone (ME) | E-mail: edizioni.universum@hotmail.it

2018.1.14　義大利國學詩
Giovanni 義大利詩評

2　森林之歌

濃密的樹林中
蝶群自成一區
在某個時辰
　振翅而出
前往雨林產卵
或者在草葉間
飛逐嬉戲
週遭是美麗的湖景
　泥土、松香和
樹蛙聲
而我所到之處
都會聽見輕柔的鳴曲
　曲聲盡是欣喜──
啊，陽光，雨水
　涓涓滴流，都是詩意

Lin Mingli/painting

−2017.12.16

2.   Song of the forest

*Dr.Lin Ming-Li

In the thick of the woods
Butterflies find their own place
At certain hour
They would fly out
To the rainforest to lay eggs
Or play in the grass
Nearby is a beautiful lake
Soil, rosin and
Sound of tree frogs
Wherever I go
I hear soft songs
Joyous music
Ah, the sunshine, the rain
The streams, all are so poetic

−2017.12.16
（Translator：Dr. William Marr）

−刊臺灣《臺灣時報》Taiwan Times，2017.12.27，圖文。
−刊美國《亞特蘭大新聞》，2017.12.29，圖文，非馬譯。

3. 當你變老

不管你信不信
我篤定
當你變老
我仍會看著月光
傳遞祝福及
　　索取一個吻
是的，我們的相知
是非比尋常的——
我常想起曾經讀過的詩
並珍藏在黝藍的星空
它讓我歡笑
　　也讓我憂愁
而你就是原因

Lin Mingli/painting

　　　−2018.1.20

3.　*When you grow old*

Dr.Lin Ming-Li

Whether you believe it or not
I am sure
When you grow old
I will still look at the moonlight
Pass on blessings and
　　Ask for a kiss
Yes, our　acquaintance
Is unusual - 一
I often think of the poems I have read
And hidden in the dark blue sky
It makes me laugh
　　It also makes me worry
And you are the reason

(Translator ：Dr. William Marr)

一刊美國《亞特蘭大新聞》，2018.02.02，
中英法及西班牙語譯，圖文，書介林明
理詩集《諦聽 LISTEN》。

法文語譯

3.　*Quand tu seras vieux*

*Dr.Lin Ming-Li

Que tu le crois ou non,

Je suis sûre

Que quand tu seras vieux

Je regarderai toujours le clair de lune,

Transmettrai mes bénédictions et

Demanderai un baiser.

Oui, notre connaissance

Est inhabituelle…

Je pense souvent aux poèmes que j'ai lus

Et que　j'ai cachés dans le ciel bleu foncé,

Ça me fait rire,

Ça me fait aussi peur

Et tu en es la raison

(Traducteur: Dr. William Marr)

Translated into French by Athanase Vantchev de Thracy

.Prof. Ernesto Kahan 於 2018/1/20 (週六) 9:53 PM MAIL 翻譯此詩 及寄來照片給林明理：

西班牙語

3.　*Cuando serás viejo*

*Dr.Lin Ming-Li

Ya sea que lo creas o no,

Estoy segura

Que cuando seas viejo

Siempre miraré la luz de la luna,

Transmitiré mis bendiciones y

　　　pediré un beso

Sí, nuestro conocimiento

Es inusual ...

A menudo pienso en los poemas que leo

Y que escondí en el cielo azul oscuro,

Eso me hace reír,

　　　También me asusta

Y tu eres el motivo

(Traducido del inglés por Ernesto Kahan)

4. 信天翁

我是逆風飛翔的歌者
不管殺人鯨或雪鳥
　　　呼嘯而過
我還是我
總離不開海上或島嶼
離不開
淨白無缺的天空

生命有時需要一點運氣
或冒險才得以生存
但生存何其不易
一切可能不如預期
或者邪惡總在
黑暗中流動
但我的歌——

有著愉悅的喧噪
不管你信不信
　　　我還是我
我喜歡獨立的思想家
他們能盡情地想像
而想像恰如我漫漫旅程中
　　　一首純真的歌

Lin Mingli/painting

　　*大多數的信天翁生活在南半球深海區域的範圍內。人們通常在大洋航行時，在海上或石礁島嶼等地方可看到信天翁。牠是世界上翅膀最長的鳥類。

-2018.1.19

4.　Albatross

*Dr. Lin Ming-Li

I am a singer flying against the wind
In spite of whales or snowbirds
　Whistling by
I'm still me
I can never do anything without the sea or islands
And cannot be separated
From the　pure white sky

Sometimes life needs a bit of luck
And adventure to survive
But survival is not　always　easy
Everything may not be as expected
Evil is constantly
Moving in the dark
But my songs ——

Have a pleasant noise
Believe it or not
　　I'm still me
I like independent thinkers
They can enjoy their imagination
And imagination is　like　a　pure song
In　my long journey

* Most albatross live in the deep-sea region of the southern hemisphere. They can usually be seen　on islands such as the Isle of Rocks,　during ocean voyage. The birds have the longest wings in the world. （Translator：Dr.William Marr）

－刊美國《亞特蘭大新聞》，2018.01.26，中英譯，非馬譯，圖文。

5. 致小說家——鄭念

在文革最黑暗之夜
妳的眼睛，清澈而幽深
吸引我眼睛朝外看的
是妳心中那盞不滅的光
　　——告訴世人
　　不要氣餒！
而我完全領會了
妳在風雨中
　　對我點頭微笑的含意

Lin Mingli/painting

　　*2018.1.30 晨間收到 Dr.William Marr 電郵一封書寫鄭念（1915-2009）的事蹟。她生於 北京，原名姚念媛，文革時被關六年，72 歲時在美國寫下一書：《 上海生死劫》《Life and Death in Shanghai》，轟動於國際，享年 94 歲。我很喜歡此則勵志 的故事，因而為詩。-2018.1.31

5.　To Novelist—Zheng Nian

*Dr. Lin Ming-Li

In the darkest night of the Cultural Revolution
Your eyes were clear and deep
What attracted me to look outward
Is the eternal light in your heart
　　—— telling the world
　"Let the past rest！"
And I fully understand　the meaning
Of your nodding at me in the storm
　　With a smile

　　*　In the morning of 2018.1.30 I received Dr.William Marr's e-mail concerning the novelist Zheng Nian (1915-2009).　Born in Beijing, formerly known as Yao Nian Yuan,　Zheng Nian was imprisoned for six years during the Cultural Revolution. At the age of 72　she published in the United States her book "Life and Death in Shanghai",　which shocked the world.　She passed away at the age of 94.

（Thraslator：Dr.William Marr）

–刊美國《亞特蘭大新聞》，2018.02.09，
中英譯，非馬　譯，圖文。

6. 請允許我分享純粹的喜悅

請允許我分享純粹的喜悅，
當暮色沉降
　　世界苦難無法舒解，
請允許我從風雪森林中
步向妳，像所有星辰，
像老橡樹靜靜守護更迭歲月。
沒錯，我將用魔法
　　把時間和空間凝結！
從現在出發──
　　且超過未來！

-2018.1.17

Lin Mingli/painting

6.　*Please allow me to share the pure joy*

*Dr. Lin Ming-Li

Please allow me to share the pure joy,
When the twilight sinks
    The suffering of the world can not be relieved,
Please allow me from the snowy forest
To walk toward you, like all the stars,
Like the old oak tree quietly guarding the years of change.
Yes, I will use magic
    To freeze time and space!
From　this point on
    And beyond the future!

（Translator：Dr. William Marr）

－刊美國《亞特蘭大新聞》，2018.02.09，
中英譯，非馬　譯，圖文。

7. 北極燕鷗

一群群，一對對
　在雲層之上
飛過高山和重洋
飛過海灣和激流
——數萬里遠，
為了生存
為了繁殖
努力向前
在南極的浮冰上越冬。
冬去春來
兩極之路，
成為他們共同的方向，
　　勇者亦如此。

Lin Mingli/painting

*北極燕鷗（The Arctic tern）是候鳥，牠們在北極繁殖，卻要飛到南極去越冬，每年在兩極之間往返一次，行程數萬公里，是世界上飛得最遠的鳥類。

-2018.1.10

7.　*The Arctic tern*

Dr. Lin Ming-Li

Flocks after　flocks
　　Above the clouds
Fly over mountains and oceans
Fly over bays and rapids
　一tens of thousands of miles　away
For survival
For breeding
They strive to move on
To pass the winter on Antarctic ice floe.
From winter to spring
The road between the South Pole　and the North pole,
Become their common direction,
　　So are the　brave.

　* The Arctic tern is a migratory bird that breeds in the Arctic and yet flies to Antarctica to wintering. It travels back and forth between the poles annually for tens of thousands of kilometers and is the farthest bird in the world.（Translator：Dr. William Marr）

2018/01/10 以色列詩人 Prof. Ernesto Kahan 於 3:05 PM MAIL
　　Dearest Ming-Li, every prize you receive produced in me,
　　an extraordinary feeling of happiness
　　I love your "The Arctic tern"　　Ernesto

法文語譯

Athanase Vantchev   MAIL2018. 1 月 20 日於 9:26 PM
Dear Mingli,
I send you the translation of your beautiful poem !

7.   *La sterne arctique*

* Dr. Lin Ming-Li

Envolées après envolées,
    Au-dessus des nuages,
Au-dessus des montagnes et des océans,
Survolant baies et rapides,
S'en vont les sternes
À des dizaines de milliers de kilomètres
Pour assurer leur survie
Et élever leurs petits.
Elles ne sont que perpétuel mouvement effréné,
Se dépêchant à passer l'hiver
Sur la banquise antarctique.
Elles parcourent,
De l'hiver au printemps,

La route entre le pôle Sud et le pôle Nord,

Route devenue le destin

De ces oiseaux si courageux !

* La sterne arctique est un oiseau migrateur qui se reproduit dans l'Arctique et qui hiverne pourtant en Antarctique. Les voyages annuels entre les deux pôles font de lui l'oiseau aux plus longs parcours.

（Translated into French by Athanase Vantchev de Thracy）

－刊美國《亞特蘭大新聞》，
2018.02.09，中英法譯，圖文。

8. 冬日的魔法

雪已融
　　露出無樹荒野
世界有時在我身上開個玩笑
而你，巨大的力量
　　　觸及我的靈魂
猶如溫暖陽光
　　讓北極大地生機盎然

-2018.1.4

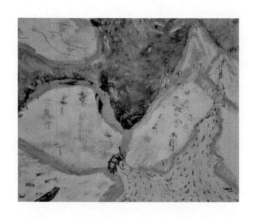

Lin Mingli/painting

8.　*Winter Magic*

* Dr. Ming-Li Lin

Snow has melted
And bared a treeless wilderness
Sometimes the world plays a trick on me
And you, great power
Touch my soul
Like a warm ray of sunshine
Vitalizes the North Polar Region

（Translator：Dr. William Marr）

－刊美國《亞特蘭大新聞》，
2018.02.16，中英譯，非馬
譯，圖文。
－刊臺灣《笠詩刊》，323 期，
2018/02，頁 61。

Prof. Ernesto Kahan
Mail 2018/01/05
於 1:45 AM
Great power = our friendship,
is mi
wonderful gift
Love

9. 你的微笑是我的微風

今年嚴冬我們遙望遠方
　談詩，相顧而笑。
你說：
你的微笑是我的微風，
　那想來就是最真的自然了。
我要說你是唯一的而我正費思
想你恰似一小片海域
　卻和廣闊的海洋相隔；
是的，我們在溫和的沙灘上走
　空氣中有海藻的味道。

-2018.2.5

Lin Mingli/painting

9. Your smile is a breeze for me

*Dr. Lin Ming-Li

All winter long we look into the far distance
Talking about poetry, smiling at each other.
You say:
Your smile is a breeze for me
That is the most natural thought.
I want to say that you are the one and only one
As a small sea space, I am thinking of
How to join your vast ocean;
Yes, we are walking on the tranquil beach
There is the smell of seaweed in the air.

（Translator：Dr. Willian Marr）

2018/02/05 ATHANASE MAIL 於 7:01 PM
Dear Mingli,

I send you the translation of your poem :

9   TON SOURIRE EST UNE BRISE POUR MOI

Tout l'hiver, nous regardions les horizons lointains,
Parlions de poésie, sourions l'un à l'autre.
Tu disais :
«Ton sourire est une brise pour moi» -
Voilà ta pensée la plus naturelle.
Je veux te dire que tu es le seul à habiter mon cœur,
Moi, petit espace maritime, je pense
Comment rejoindre ton vaste océan;
Oui, nous marchions sur la plage tranquille,
Il y avait l'odeur d'algues dans l'air.

(Translated into French by Athanase Vantchev de Thracy)

←圖 9-1　　　　↑圖 9-2

－刊美國《亞特蘭大新聞》，2018.02.16，中英法譯，圖文。
－刊臺灣《大海洋詩雜誌》，LARGE OCEAN POETRY
　QUARTERLY.第 97 期，2018.07，頁 87，非馬英譯。
* 2018/02/09　prof. Ernesto Kahan MAIL 2:40 PM

Estoy feliz con nuestra amistad
que nos eleva por encima de las canciones.
El suelo se cubre de flores perfumadas
los poemas son ondas de mensajes
el mundo acuático de las pinturas
florece en las manos de Mingli
el colibrí de mi jardín nos festeja
y yo camino sonriendo

10. 你在哪？孩子

你在哪？孩子
媽媽在等你
你可曉得
救難員急著尋找地點
在黝黑星空下寒冷
在斷垣殘壁中淒涼
連雲影也哽咽了。
我愛你
還是和以前一樣，一切未變
不要怕，我的寶貝；

Lin Mingli/painting

在這夜晚的寂靜中
我明白了，
你有話對我說…
我會為你祈禱
也為和我一樣在這裡守候的
所有人家，
願諸神聽到我們
在渴求，在呼喚———
讓我們肩並肩
擦乾淚水，再闊步向前。

*為紀念 2018 年 2 月 6 日花蓮強震而作。罹難者小軒母親
　的焦慮與心碎的畫面，催人心肝。願天佑花蓮，全民一
　心加入救助行列與同悼。　　　　　　　－2018.2.8

10　*where are you? My child*

*Dr. Lin Ming-Li

where are you? my child
Mom is waiting for you
You know
Rescuers are trying desperately to find you
It is cold under the dark sky
The broken wall is so desolate
That even the low clouds feel choked.
I love you
Still, as always, nothing has changed
Do not be afraid, my baby

In the silence of the night
I understand,
You have something to say to me ...
I will pray for you
There are also people waiting here like me
May the gods hear
our prayers
Let us stand side by side
Dry our tears, then   stride forward.

—刊臺灣《華文現代詩》，十七期，2018.05，頁七十五。—美國《亞特蘭大新聞》，2018.02.16，中英譯，非馬譯，圖文。

* To commemorate the earthquake in Hualien on February 6, 2018. Xuanxuan mothers of the victims of anxiety and heart broken picture, inspiring. God willing to bless Hualian, the whole nation bent on joining the ranks of relief and the same mourning.
—2018.2.8（Translator：Dr. Willia m Marr）

11. 麥田圈之謎

一個光球
　　靜靜地
在地表上
留下了力與美的圖騰
誰能解開它的謎題
誰就能打開探索宇宙之鑰
啊可悲的人類
　　　以核武耀威
讓地球之臉日顯憔悴
讓外星生物急於傳遞
　　警訊

－2018.1.29

Lin Mingli/painting

11. The Mistery of Crop Circles

*Dr. Lin Ming-Li

A flaring ball
　　quietly
Left　on the earth
An imprint of　power and beauty
Who can solve the mistery?
Who can open the lock to explore the universe
Ah pitiful　human　beings
　　Foolishly waving nuclear weapons
Making the face of the earth　haggard

causing　alien　creatures
rush over　to　deliver
　　warning　messages

（Translator：Dr. William Marr）

－刊美國《亞特蘭大新聞》，
　2018.02.16，中英譯，非馬
　譯，圖文。

12. 夕陽落在沙丘之後

數百隻鵜鶘飛起
飛進那寒冷的海岸，
回到那入海的泥地
整個冬天都將繁殖著。
而艾爾湖湖面和鹽盤，、
讓我的思緒隨之而去；
我願是
桉樹下乘涼的野馬那樣生活。
在我所選擇的方向奔跑，
微笑地站著，好像整片天空
——屬我一個。

　　* 艾爾湖 Lake Eyre，
　　　是澳洲最大鹹水湖。

　　－201/8.2.6

Lin Mingli/painting

12. Sunset behind the dunes

* Dr. Lin Ming-Li

Hundreds of pelicans fly up
And into the cold coast,
Back to the mud basin at the entrance to the sea
To breed during the winter.
The surface and salt plates of Lake Eyre
Carry my thoughts away;
I wish I could live
Like the wild horses under the Eucalyptus.
Run in the direction of my choice,
Stand with a smile, as if the whole sky
belongs to me.

* Lake Eyre is the largest lagoon in Australia.

（Translator：Dr. William Marr）

2018.2.6 今天 prof. Ernesto Kahan 於 9:59 PM Mail
I will wait for your new book with a great expectation
This poem about pelicans is very sweet.
Love
Ernesto

Athanase　2018.2.8MAIL 於 3:01 AM Mail

法文語譯

12. Coucher de soleil derrière les dunes

Des centaines de pélicans s'envolent
Vers la côte froide,
Ils retournent au bassin de boue à l'entrée de la mer
Pour se reproduire pendant l'hiver.
La surface recouverte de plaques de sel du lac Eyre
Emportent mes pensées loin de moi :
J'aimerais pouvoir vivre
Comme les chevaux sauvages sous les eucalyptus.
Courir partout où je veux,
M'arrêter et sourire comme si le ciel entier
M'appartenait.

> * Le lac Eyre est le plus grand lac salé d'Australie.
> （Translated into French by Athanase Vantchev de Thracy）

2018.2/15　今天　於　7:16 PM Hi Mingli, grazie per l'invio. H o tradotto una tua poesia in italiano. Dimmi se ti piace. Un abbraccio Giovanni

義大利語

12　TRAMONTO DIETRO LE DUNE

Dr. Lin Ming-Li

Centinaia di pellicani
volano dalla fredda costa,
verso il delta del mare
per nidificare durante l'inverno.
La superficie piatta e salata del
　Lago Eyre,
cattura i miei pensieri.
Vorrei poter vivere
come cavallo selvaggio sotto
　gli eucalipti,
correre in direzione della mia
　scelta,
essere sorridente, come se tutto
　il cielo
appartenesse a me.

Il Lago Eyre è la laguna più grande dell'Australia.
Traduttore: Giovanni G. Campisi

－刊於義大利《國際詩新聞 IPN》INTERNATIONAL POETRY NEWS，2018/02/15，中文及義大利語，Giovanni G. Campisi 譯。
－刊美國《亞特蘭大新聞》，2018/02/23，中英法譯，圖文。
－刊臺灣《大海洋詩雜誌》，LARGE OCEAN POETRY QUARTERLY. 第 97 期，2018. 07，頁 87，非馬英譯。

13. 當濃霧散去

一隻兀鷲
從安地斯山脈某一角落
　　　　疾飛。
濃霧散去，
鹽灘和冰原底下，
每種生物都習常的
　　　為生存而奮鬥。
七千公里，
　山河橫亙，
眾鳥聒噪，
　　　越過白晝與黑夜。
我感知，
在雲霞棲息處，牠展翼
　　宛如天使，
或者——牠悄然離去，
或者——深情回應我的注視。

Lin Mingli/painting

－2018.1.22

13. When the dense fog dispersed

*Dr. Lin Ming-Li

A vulture
From some corner of the Andes
　　Fly rapidly.
Dense fog dispersed,
Under the salt flats and ice sheets,
All creatures
　　Strive for survival.
Across seven thousand kilometers
Of mountains and rivers,
　　Day and night,
Birds clamor
I can feel
In the clouds, it spreads its wings
　　Like an angel,
Either —— it leaves quietly,
Or —— affectionately responds to my gaze.

（Translator：Dr. William Marr）

2018.01.23 Athanase 於 8:49 PM MAIL
Dear Mingli, I translated this poem into French :

13. QUAND LE BROUILLARD DENSE S'EST DISPERSÉ

* Dr. Lin Ming-Li

Un vautour
Des Andes
          Vole à grande vitesse !
Le brouillard dense s'est dispersé.
Dans les salines et sous les calottes glaciaires,
Toutes les créatures
          S'efforcent à survivre.
Tout le long de sept mille kilomètres,
Dans les montagnes et dans les rivières,
J'entends,
Nuit et jour,
La clameur des oiseaux.
Ils déploient leurs ailes dans les nuages
Comme des anges –

Tantôt ils s'envolent tranquillement,
Tantôt ils répondent avec grâce
À mon regard plein d'affection !

(Traducteur: Dr. William Marr)

（Translated into French by Athanase Vantchev
de Thracy）

－刊美國《亞特蘭大新聞》，2018/02/23，
中英法譯，圖文。

14. 致吾友－prof. Ernesto Kahan

巨大的冰河
也無法消融我的銘記。
你神奇地出現
激起所有思想的漣漪，
如冰晶之中的幻影
似原野樹梢的雪花；
你對我說的每句輕聲細語，
　讓我生命帶有
色彩、笑容和明燦的未來。

－2018/2/17

Lin Mingli/painting

14　To my friend－prof. Ernesto Kahan

*Dr. Lin Ming-Li

Even the giant glacier

Can't wipe out my memory.

Your magical appearance

Stirs up ripples of my thoughts,

Like the illusion in the ice crystals

Or the snow on treetops in the wilderness;

Your every soft whisper to me

Renders color, smile and bright future

　　To my life

（Translator：Dr.William Marr）

2018/2/17 prof .Ernesto Kahan 於 7:57 PM mail
I really want to see and feel...
your rose garden
velvet petals
caressed beach sand
by the waves of the blue sea
where the seagulls rest
of the magestuoso flight
When your perfumes call me
when they return from the great dance
of my dream
2018/2/21 ATHANASE MAIL 於 7:55 PM
Good morning, dear Mingli,

Here is the translation of your poem:

14　À MON AMI ERNESTO

Même un glacier géant

Ne peut effacer les images de ma mémoire.

Ton apparence magique

Provoque les divagations de mes pensées,

Et tout en moi

Est comme une illusion née au cœur des cristaux de glace,

Comme de la neige sur les cimes des arbres en plein désert ;

Ton doux murmure rend mon avenir brillant

Et plein de couleurs et de sourires.

（Translated into French by Athanase Vantchev de Thracy）

－刊美國《亞特蘭大新聞》，2018/03/02，中英法譯，圖文。

2018/03/03 Ernesto 於 3:42 PM Mail
Mingli,
You are devine
for ever
for ever love
pure heart
pure poetry of colour and nature.
never ending mountains of colours
in your hands and...
... in my eyes and heart for ever

15. 戰爭仍茫無盡頭

如同盲魚在無止境的
黑暗中，
戰爭仍茫無盡頭。
為何戰機轟擊了我的家？
為何連醫院也被摧毀？
為何敘利亞天空之雲
　　飄浮得如此沉重？
我們的每一步都走在歷史上，
難民的嚴冬，風徹夜蕭瑟。

　　　－2018.1.19

15. The war still no end in sight

* Dr. Lin Ming-Li

Like a blind fish
in the endless darkness,
The war is still no end in sight.
Why the fighter jet bombarded my home?
Why even the hospital was destroyed?
Why the clouds in the Syrian sky
　　Floating so heavily?
Our every step becomes history,
In the winter of the refugees, the wind blowing all night .

（Translator Dr. William Marr）

－刊美國《亞特蘭大新聞》，2018/03/02，中
英譯，非馬譯。

Giovanni G. Campisi / Italian poet

16. 給 Giovanni G. Campisi

吾友，當你沉靜的目光
觸碰到我的詩園時，
我認出了
你祖先堅韌的血液及
熱情的靈魂；
並因此而讓我更瞭解
你在我身邊，友情不移。

Giovanni G. Campisi

* 2018/2/16 於 5:21 AM Italian poet Giovanni
  G. Campisi
  Mail Mingli Lin 祝賀明理 2018 中國新年快樂，
  有感而詩。
  －2018/2/16

Hi Mingli,
grazie per tutte le cose belle che mi scrivi.
AUGURI PER IL NUOVO ANNO!!!
Come regalo, ti mando la mia foto.
Spero che ti piaccia.
Un grande abbraccio a te e alla tua famiglia.

Giovanni

16.　To Giovanni G. Campisi

*Dr. Lin Ming-Li

My friend, when your quiet eyes
Are directed to my poetry garden,
I come to realize
The tough blood and the passionate
Soul of your ancestors;
And I know more clearly
With you by my side, our friendship lasts.

（Translator：Tianjin Normal University
professor Zhang Zhizhong）

－刊美國《亞特蘭大新聞》，2018/03/02，
中英譯，天津師範大學外語系張智中教
授英譯。

2018/2/21 於 6:26 AMMAIL MINGLI
Ciao Mingli,
grazie per la bellissima poesia.
La pubblicherò sul prossimo IPN.
Un abbraccio
Giovanni

法文語譯

2018/3/11MAIL 於 9:00 PM
My dear Mingli, my dear Poetesse,

Thank you for your messages. I translated a new poem and send it to you !
Have a nice time !
Athanase

16. À Giovanni G. Campisi

* Dr. Lin Mingli

Mon ami, quand tes regards calmes

Se tournent vers mon jardin de poésie,

Je reconnais immédiatement

Le sang dur, le sang passionné

Et l'âme de tes ancêtres.

Je suis sûre

Que tu es à mes côtés

Et que notre amitié durera.

2018/3/1 於 6:02 AM Giovanni e-mail
Ciao Mingli,

grazie per la traduzione in francese della mia poesia di Athanase.

In questi giorni ho molto lavoro e poche energie per lavorare.

Appena posso, ti scriverò una bellissima poesia.

Un abbraccio.

Giovanni

17. 向亞城許月芳主編致意

讓我們忘記時間
在新的一年裡
不斷向前
這世界
很多文化逐漸消失
很多世道崎嶇難行
讓我們再一次
航向未知
世界何其寬廣
有太多值得去探索
我們不能錯過
讓我們攜手共赴
而您的堅持——
亞城，也因而顯得獨特

Lin Mingli/painting

　　註：許月芳，金門人，離鄉赴美定居數十年，擔任亞
　　　　特蘭大新聞主編及社長一職，每期報刊分送當地
　　　　圖書館，以供華人免費閱讀，常舉辦書香會等活
　　　　動，促進海外華界文藝交流，因而為詩致意。

　　－2018/2/23

17. Tribute to Yue Fang editor

* Dr. Lin Ming-Li

Let us forget the time
In the new year
Keep moving forward
this world
Many cultures are gradually disappearing
A lot of troubled world hard
Let us again
The heading is unknown
How broad the world
There is too much to explore
We can not miss it
Let's go hand in hand
And your insistence——
Atlanta City, and thus seem unique

－刊美國《亞特蘭大新聞》亞城園地，
　2018/03/02，中英譯。2018/07/06.

2018.7.6 Ming-Li

－刊臺灣《金門日報》副刊，2018./06/29。

18. 長　城

他，日日夜夜
從塔樓望穿山陵線
聆聽著———
曾經窮盡一切
而流下的血淚故事
那些都覆蓋在蜿蜒的夜影
與夢中，不再有悔憾了

－2018/3/1

Lin Mingli/painting

18. *The Great Wall*

*Dr. Lin Ming-Li

He, day and night
Looks from the tower through the mountain ridge line
Listens to
After exhausting everything
The remaining bloody stories
Which are covered by the meandering night shadows
And dreams, no longer feels any regret

（Translator Dr. William Marr）

－刊美國《亞特蘭大新聞》，2018/03/09，
中英譯，非馬譯。
－刊臺灣（大海洋詩雜誌），第 98 期，
2019/01，頁 19。

19. 為搶救童妓而歌

那孩子……
被迫在火坑裡
長大。
她可能來自悲慘的
歲月，來自失去滿臉稚氣的
童年。
那孩子……沒有選擇的
自由；暗夜哭泣於其中，
舔拭傷口於其中，
那孩子吶喊著
　　──神的名字，
隨後只有窗櫺的風作伴，
聲音越來越微弱
熄滅於黑暗的角落中。
啊，哪裡有光？
哪裡能更親近神的國度？
那孩子只想在
　　陽光下盪鞦韆…
甜甜地一笑。

Lin Mingli/painting

－2018/3/1

19. Child prostitution

*Dr. Lin Ming-Li

The kid ...
Forced to grow up
in the firepit.
She might have come from a tragic
Time, from the loss of innocent
childhood.
The child ... has no choice
But to cry in dark nights,
Licking her wounds.
But only the wind outside the window
responded
With a fading sound...
Into the dark corner.
Ah, where is the light?
Where can I get near God's kingdom?
The kid just wants to be there
Playing on a swing under the sun ...
With a sweet smile.

－刊美國《亞特蘭大新聞》，2018/03/09，中英譯，非馬譯。

（Translator：Dr. William Marr）

20. 在遠方的巴列姆山谷

地表上的達尼人小孩
　　在野果中
　　在夜空下
　　　　甜甜地睡去
母親為他蓋上了被子。
狂野的河浪，山豬的蹤跡
　　…都離得遠遠的…
美麗的花兒啊
　　在河邊綻放

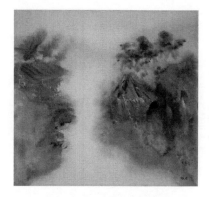

Lin Mingli/painting

勇士們把獵物牢牢放好。
他們汲水而歌，燧石而舞
　　遠離煩囂；
而我深信
百年以後這美妙的山谷
在紅薯梯田
與陡峭的山峰之間，
仍有部落歌舞著——恰似
　　時光在歌唱。

　　＊ 巴列姆山谷（Baliem Valley）位於印尼巴布亞省的中
　　　央山脈裡，為海拔 1600 多米的天然山谷。－2018.2.5

20.　In the remote Balmain Valley

*Dr. Lin Ming-Li

On the ground ＿ in the middle of　wild fruits
　　A Dani child　is having a sweet　dream
　　Under the night sky
His mother puts　a blanket over him.
Wild　river current, traces of mountain pigs
　　　are　all far away　...
Beautiful flowers
　　Bloom on the riverbank
Warriors put away their hunting catches .
They sing while drawing water, dance while chipping rocks
　　Far away from hustle and bustle
And I am convinced
A hundred years from now this wonderful valley
In the sweet potato terraces
Between steep peaks,
There remain tribal songs and dances —— just like
　　Time is singing.

（Translator：Dr. William Marr）
－刊美國《亞特蘭大新聞》，2018/03/09，中英譯，非馬譯，圖文。

21. 寄　語

你的詩如是輕盈，
我把它寄予飛燕，
不管穿越多少千里，
已開啓想念之門。

-2018/3/6

Lin Mingli/painting

21.　*Message*

*Dr. Lin Ming-Li

Your poetry is so slim and graceful,

I send it to the swallows,

Regardless of how many thousands of miles they fly,

The door of yearning is always open.

（Translator：Dr. William Marr）
－刊美國《亞特蘭大新聞》，2018.03.16，
中英譯，非馬譯，圖文。

2018/03/17 ATHANASE　MAIL 於 8:37 PM
My dear Mingli,

I send you the translation of your beautiful little poem :

法文語譯

21.　Message

Votre poésie est si fine, si gracieuse,
Je l'offre en pâture aux hirondelles,
Peu importe les milliers de kilomètres
Qu'elles ont parcourus,
La porte de la soif d'harmonie
Reste toujours ouverte.

（Translator：Athanase Vantchev de Thracy）

22. 鯨之舞

一尾座頭鯨
在大海上展放歌喉
二十哩外
一隻母鯨隨著歌聲跳起華爾滋……
寰宇靜寂，
彷彿
只剩這對珍奇的生物，
　在一個幸福的國度裡旋舞。

－2018.03.07

Lin Mingli/painting

22.　*Dance of The whales*

*Lin Ming-Li

A humpback whale
Sings in the sea
Twenty miles away
A female whale dances with the song...
The world is so quiet and peaceful,
As if
Only this pair of rare creatures remain,
　Waltzing happily together.

　　　　　－2018.03.7

　　（Translator：Dr. William Marr）

　　－刊美國《亞特蘭大新聞》，2018/03/16，
　　中英譯，非馬譯，圖文。

23. ——用心說話

我深信
在巨大的黑暗空間，
　或宇宙的某處
　　也有生物存在。
人們多以功利的觀點看待世界，
卻忽略去尋找我們存在的道路。
珊瑚礁生物為下一代而
　　竭盡所能，
　為尋找伴侶而
長途跋涉或深入險境。
在深海僅有的微光裡，
遺世獨立，
如今，地球暖化及過度捕魚，
藍色珊瑚礁...一片片...
遂成荒涼的廢墟，
　　海底居民也無家可歸。

Lin Mingli/painting

23. —— speak in heart

*Dr. Lin Ming-Li

I am convinced

That in the huge dark space,

Or somewhere in the universe

Other creatures also exist.

Most people view the world from a utilitarian point of view,

And neglect to find   the way of coexistence.

The living things in the coral reefs do everything they can

For their next generation.

In the search of a partner

They take long journey and dive into dangerous depth

To survive.

Now that the planet is warming up and also because of overfishing,

The blue coral reefs are falling apart, piece by piece

And turned into desolate ruins.

Submarine residents

啊　白化的珊瑚，終將死亡，

無知的人類，猶為掠奪

　或核戰而加速滅絕。

　　　　　＊ 科學家預期，到 21 世紀末期時，地
　　　　　球的珊瑚礁可能成為絕跡。

　　　　　－2018.1.26

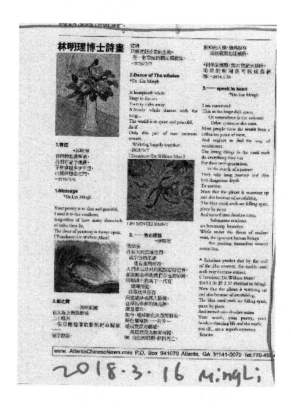

are becoming   homeless

While under the threat of nuclear wars, the ignorant human beings

Are pushing themselves toward extinction.

* Scientists predict that by the end of the 21st century, the earth's coral reefs may become extinct.

（Translator：Dr. William Marr）

－刊美國《亞特蘭大新聞》，2018/03/16，中英譯，非馬譯，圖文。

*2018.1.26 於 2:37 PM prof. Ernesto Kahan Mail to Mingli
Now that the planet is warming up and also because of overfishing,
The blue coral reefs are falling apart, piece by piece
And turned into desolate ruins.
Your words, your poetry, your hands embracing life and the truths,
you all... are a   superb existence

Ernesto

24.　別哭泣，敘利亞小孩

別哭泣，孩子。
　我用掌心觸碰你蒼白之臉，
　我以沉痛寫出戰爭無情的詩篇。
你說，流亡扼殺了我們，
你說，只能在睡夢中或
　　　只能透過想像夢想著夢，
你說，敘利亞是永遠的故鄉，
　　　但故鄉何其遠？
只有唯一真實的月光
才能無懼地說出心底的思念。
你說砲聲響過，坦克車來了！
　　　為什麼要不停地殺害我們？
啊......你短短的問話，
　　讓大地同悲，眾神也無言。

　　　＊ 據統計，流亡難民的時間可能長達十七年。

　　　－2018.1.18

24.　Don't cry, Syrian child

* Dr. Lin Ming-Li

Don't cry, my boy.

　I touched your pale face with my palm,

　Painfully I write a poem about the cruel war.

You say exile has strangled you,

You say, only in sleep or

　　In your dream can you dream,

You say Syria is your home forever,

　　But how far away is your hometown?

Only the moon

Can tell you without any fear.

You say the guns roar, the tanks roll!

　　Why they keep trying to kill you?

Ah …… your brief question,

　Makes the earth sad, and the gods speechless.

（Translator： Dr. William Marr）

* According to statistics, the average time for refugees in exile may be as long as 17 years.

－刊美國《亞特蘭大新聞》，2018/06/01，中英譯，非馬譯。

－刊臺灣《文學台灣》季刊，第106期，2018/04，夏季號，頁118。

25. 悲傷的小企鵝

早安，美麗的海洋！
　荒涼的冬日
　悄悄爬過我翅膀，
我夢見
從海冰的前緣
　走向自己的部落。
風沉默了
鳥不再成群聒叫，
我閉著眼睛，發出哀鳴
耳邊聽海鳥之聲。
在這無盡苦寒的季節
我仍聽得見娘親…遠遠地
　…哼著歌。

Lin Mingli/painting

　　＊ 據 2017 年報導，南極生態大浩劫，千
　　隻企鵝寶寶只剩 2 隻。冰棚瓦解加速，企
　　鵝的未來堪慮。
　－2018./01/12.

25　Sad little penguins

* Dr. Lin Ming-Li

Good morning, beautiful ocean!
　The desolate winter day
　Is quietly climbing over my wings,
I dream　of　walking
From the front edge of the ice
　To my own tribe.
The wind is silent
Birds no longer cry in hordes
I close my eyes and whine
In this endless, bitterly cold season
I can still hear my mother ... in the　distance
　... humming a song.

　* According to reports in 2017,　only two penguins have survived the Antarctic ecological catastrophe.　With the speedup　of the collapse of the ice sheet, the penguins have a worrisome　future indeed.
　（Translator：Dr. William Marr）
　－刊美國《亞特蘭大新聞》，2018/03/30，中英譯，非馬譯，圖文。
　－刊臺灣《臺灣時報》，台灣文學版，2018/03/14，圖文。

2018./01/25ATHANASE 的法詩 MAIL 於 10:50 PM

25. TRISTES PETITS PINGOUINS

* Dr. Lin Ming-Li

Bonjour, magnifique océan !

Le jour désolé de l'hiver

Est en train de grimper tranquillement sur mes ailes,

Je rêve de marcher

Du bord de ce plateau de glace

Jusqu'à ma tribu.

Le vent est silencieux,

Les hordes des oiseaux ne pleurent plus,

Je ferme les yeux et gémis

Dans cette saison amère et d'un froid infini,

Je peux encore entendre ma mère ... au loin

... Fredonner une chanson !

* Selon les rapports de 2017, seuls deux pingouins ont survécu à la catastrophe écologique antarctique. Avec l'accélération de l'effondrement de la calotte glaciaire, les pingouins ont en effet un avenir inquiétant.

（Traduit en français par Athanase Vantchev de Thracy）

*2018./0 1/12 日於 11:33 PM Ernesto mail
Hoy amaneciste en el polo,

con los pinguinos, Mingli

y yo me dije
- Eres señal
de poesía ecológica y nueva miel -

Eres la música que me atrapa

Today you woke up at the polo,
with the penguins, Mingli

and I told myself
- You are a signal
of ecological poetry and new honey -

You are the music that catches me

26. 季雨來了

所有島嶼不約而同地發聲
所有生物都在唱和——
在婆羅洲熱帶雨林中，
如你有雙好眼睛
　　又能聽見魚群的舞蹈
豬籠草的捕誘，樹鼩的竊笑
　　　海龜也在漫遊著...
啊，我是我命運的主宰
我做我想要的
　　——自由和冒險；
而感受大自然的美妙也將
　　隨之而來。

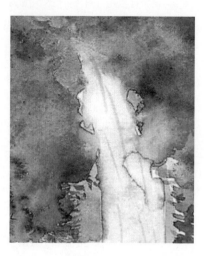

Lin Mingli/painting

　＊　婆羅洲（馬來語：Borneo），是世界
　　　第三大島，亞洲第一大島。
　－2018.2.3

26. The Seasonal Rain Is Coming

* Dr. Lin Ming-Li

Spontaneously all islands sing

And all creatures sing along——

In the tropical rainforest of Borneo,

If you have a pair of good eyes

    And can hear the dancing   fish

the trapping Nepenthes, the snickering tree shrews

    And the roaming sea turtles ...

Ah, I am the master of my destiny

I do what I want

    ——free and adventurous;

And the feeling of natural beauty will follow.

* Borneo (Malay: Borneo) is the third largest island in the world and the largest island in Asia.（Translator：Dr. William Marr）

－刊美國《亞特蘭大新聞》，2018/03/23，中英法譯，圖文。

*收件者 2018 年 2 月 3 日於 10:13 PM
Thanks my lovely Mingli. Beautiful picture and poem
Ernesto

法文語譯

2018.2.4ATHANASE 於 7:00 PM MAIL
Good morning, dear Mingli,
Thank you for your message. I send you the translation of
your poem :

26.　La pluie saisonnière arrive

Spontanément toutes les îles chantent

Et toutes les créatures chantent ...

Dans la forêt tropicale de Bornéo,

Si vous avez une paire de bons yeux,

Si vous pouvez écouter

Vous entendrez   le poisson dansant,

Les nepenthes piégeurs,

Les musaraignes d'arbre qui ricanent

Et les tortues de mer errantes ...

Ah, si je suis maître de mon destin,

Je ferai ce que je voudrai

—— je serai libre et aventureux ;

Alors le sentiment de beauté naturelle suivra.

(Traducteur: Dr. William Marr)

（Translated into French by Athanase Vantchev de Thracy）

27. 我一直在看著你

我看見一顆星子在懸崖上
在這冬季 黑夜
俯視我眼底的深情。

我看見一小苔蘚在瀑布旁
感覺到越是稀少的物種
在自然界裡越難以親近。

Lin Mingli/painting

我看見冰層逐年融化，消失。
生命短暫。我
卻一直想這樣看著你，永遠幸福。

　　　　　－2018.03.10

27. I've always been watching you

*Dr. Lin Ming-Li

I see a star on the cliff
At this winter night
Overlooking the deep affections in my eyes.

I see a small moss next to the waterfall
The rarer species in nature
The more difficult to get close in nature.

I see the ice layer melting and disappearing year after year.
Life is so short
I want to look at you like this, ever so happy.

（Translator：Dr. William Marr）

－刊臺灣《秋水》詩刊 CHIU SHUI POETRY QUARTERLY，176 期，2018/07，頁 72。

－刊美國《亞特蘭大新聞》，2018/03/30，中英譯，非馬譯，圖文。

28. 我將獨行

多少次
我們走過這小徑，
月寂寂。山脈諦聽著海音，
夜鷺緩踱。

大海看似平靜，
肥沃的田野睡在星輝中。
總是相視、無語，
細碎的足聲踏響整個天際。

Lin Mingli/painting

今日，我將獨行
──依然走在這條舊路，
你已遠去，而我心悠悠；
重逢是未來歲月的憂愁。

$-$2018.03.18

28. I will walk alone

*Dr. Lin Ming-Li

How many times
Have we walked through this trail,
The moon is silent, the mountains are listening to
the sound of the sea,
A night heron paces slowly.

The sea seems calm,
The fertile fields sleep soundly in the starlight.
Always looking at each other, wordless,
The sound of our　footsteps echoes across the sky.

Today, I will walk alone
　——on this old trail,
You are gone, and my heart is pensive;
Reunion is the worries of the future.

（Translator：Dr. William Marr）

－刊美國《亞特蘭大新聞》，2018/03/30，
中英譯，非馬譯，圖文。

29. 美麗的冰山

大翅鯨，浮出水面
掀起波浪，
忽而是充氣艇泛過，
企鵝、海豹，
還有孤岩上的甚麼。
啊，閉上眼，
就能看見在島嶼和海洋間
那最遠處——
　是地表上最美的天堂！

－2018/3/3

Lin Mingli/painting

29.　The Beautiful iceberg

*Dr. Lin Ming-Li

A whale, rose to the surface
Raising the waves
Soon an air boat zoomed by
Then the penguins, seals,
And whatever were on the skerry.
Ah, close your eyes,
You can then see between the island and the ocean
That farthest place —
　The most beautiful paradise on earth!

（Translator：Dr. William Marr）

－刊美國《亞特蘭大新聞》，2018.04.
　06，中英譯，非馬譯，圖文。

－刊臺灣《臺灣時報》，台灣文學版，
　2018/04/18，圖文。

30. 奔騰的河流

在你無羈的蛇行中
　從源頭來到出海口
有許多部落棲息著。
我像匹馬
　　豎耳傾聽，
那昏暗的林冠層下
　是雨林和沼澤，
有鼓聲喧響
——族人歡舞；
　分享古老的傳說。

Lin Mingli/painting

哦，奔騰的河流
　鹹水鱷的出沒
　峽谷的濃霧
　種子的呼吸
　禽鳥展翼之中
我想跟著你奔跑
　　跳躍；

30. *Torrential Stream*

*Dr. Lin Ming-Li

Stretching like a snake
　　From the source to the entrance of the sea
There are many tribal inhabitants.
I, like a horse
　　　Listen to the drumbeats,
Under the dark canopy
The clans are dancing,
　　Sharing an ancient legend.

Oh, torrential stream
　　The appearance and disappearance
　　Of salt water crocodiles
　　Dense fog in the canyon
　　The breath of seeds
　　The flapping wings of birds
I want to run with you
　　　And jump;

未來的困難是不可避免的，
但沒有目標，
　　就不算是英雄。

－2018/02/07

－刊美國《亞特蘭大新聞》，2018/04/06，
　中英譯，非馬譯，圖文。
－刊臺灣《華文現代詩》Chinese modern
　poetry Quarterly，第 17 期，2018/05，頁
　75。

Future difficulties are inevitable,

But without a　goal

　　There won't be any hero.

*2018 年 2 月　8　日於 10:21 PM　ERNESTO　MAIL
I love the poem, very much

*2018/02/09　ERNESTO MAIL 2:40 PM

Estoy feliz con nuestra amistad

que nos eleva por encima de las canciones.

El suelo se cubre de flores perfumadas

los poemas son ondas de mensajes

el mundo acuático de las pinturas

florece en las manos de Mingli

el colibrí de mi jardín nos festeja

y yo camino sonriendo

31. 愛的宣言

這看起來是必然的，
就算穿越時空
也無法再那樣瘋狂
　　甚而愛上你。
愛，它需要一點奇蹟，
一點冒險，
　　加上一些勇氣；
哪怕從叢林到沙漠，
從黑海沿岸到太平洋，
我都在初遇的橄欖山
　　──等著你。

Lin Mingli/painting

－2018.3.25

31. Declaration of love

* Dr. Lin Ming-Li

It seems inevitable.

Even across time and space

There's no way that can make me so crazy

as to love you.

Love, it takes a little miracle,

A little adventure,

Add some courage;

Even from the jungle to the desert,

From the coast of the Black Sea to the Pacific,

I will wait for you at the Olive Hill

——where I first met you.

－2018.3.25

（Translator：Dr. William Marr）

－刊美國《亞特蘭大新聞》，2018/04/06，
中英譯，非馬譯，圖文。
－刊美國《亞特蘭大新聞》，2018/07/06，
中、法、義大利語譯，圖文。

*Ernesto mail2018 年 3 月 25 日於 11:19 PM
Mingli,
This is the most beautiful poem letter I can receive.
　Your words are like a magic perfume.
Thanks my beautiful dear

法文語譯

2018 年 5 月 21 日 ATHANASE MAIL 於 6:38 PM
Dear Ming-Li,

Thank you from the bottom of my heart. Thank you for your
support ! Very tender bouquet of flowers !
　I send you the translation into French of your poem :

31.　Déclaration d'amour

Cela semble inévitable.
Rien à travers l'espace et le temps
Ne peut me rendre folle
Et m'interdire de t'aimer.
L'Amour ? Il faut un petit miracle,
Une petite aventure,
Un peu de courage pour l'atteindre !
De la jungle au désert,
De la côte de la mer Noire aux côtes du Pacifique,
Je t'attendrai à l'Olive Hill
Là où je t'ai rencontré pour la première fois.

Dr. Lin Ming-Li　　　　　　　－2018.3.25
（Translator：Athanase Vantchev de Thracy）

義大利語譯

2018 年 6 月 28 日 Giovanni 於 下午 8:40 MAIL

Hi Ming-Li,

I loved your poem "DECLARATION OF LOVE" and so I translated it into Italian.

I hope you like it.

A big hug.

Giovanni

25-03-2018

31. DICHIARAZIONE D'AMORE

Lin Ming-Li

Mi sembra inevitabile.

Anche attraverso il tempo e lo spazio,

non c'è cosa che mi fa impazzire,

come l'amore per te.

Per amare, ci vuole un piccolo miracolo,

una piccola avventura,

Aggiungi un po'di coraggio;

anche dalla giungla al deserto,

dalla costa del Mar Nero al Pacifico,

ti aspetterò al Monte degli Ulivi

dove prima ti ho incontrato.

(Tradotta da Giovanni Campisi)

西班牙語譯

2018.7.12 Giovanni MAIL   Hi Ming-Li,

Your poem "DECLARATION OF LOVE" translated into Spanish now and published in an anthology together with authors from all over the world.

Today I received your beautiful book, I like it so much.

Can you send me another exemplar for Sara Ciampi?

Let me know.   Giovanni

31.   *DECLARACIÓN DE AMOR*

Me parece inevitable.

también a través del tiempo y el espacio,

no hay nada que me vuelva loco,

como el amor por ti

Para amar, se necesita un pequeño milagro,

una pequeña aventura,

Agregue algo de coraje

también desde la jungla hasta el desierto,

desde la costa del Mar Negro hasta el Pacífico.

Te esperaré en el Monte de los Olivos

donde te conocí por primera vez

(Tradotta da Giovanni Campisi)

LIN MING-LI – TAIWAN   (R. O.C.)

32. Google＋

這裡藏有我的夢想；圖文天地，
認識地球村友人、自然和動物，
是開啓我學習攝影的居所。

－2018/03/29

林明理攝影 / 圖

32.   *Google* +

*Dr. Lin Ming-Li

My dreams are stored here, as well as my paintings.

I meet my global village friends here, as well as
nature and animals,

It is also my home to learn photography.

（Translator：Dr. William Marr）

－刊美國《亞特蘭大新聞》，2018/04/13，中
英譯，非馬譯，圖文。

33. 朋友

　　——就像北極星，
　　無論我身處何地，
　　永遠知道彼此的距離。
　　無須鉅細靡遺地訴說，
　　沒有妒嫉，沒有猜疑，
　　在我心中閃耀著
　　　澄澈溫柔的記憶。

　　　　　　　－2018/03/20

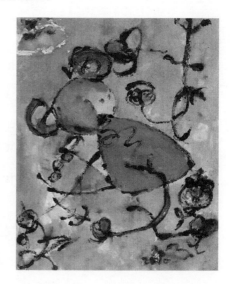

Lin Mingli/painting

33.　Friend

*Dr. Lin Ming-Li

Like Polaris,
No matter where I am,
We always know our distance.
There is no need to say in detail,
No jealousy, no suspicion,
Shining in my heart
Are clear and tender memories.

（Translator：Dr. William Marr）

－刊美國《亞特蘭大新聞》，
2018/04/13，中英譯，非馬譯，
圖文。

34. 山野的蝴蝶

你是否來自遙遠的國度？
　和我一樣，自由放任，
飄過遠古的陸地，神秘的山谷，
從崎嶇的海岸奔向福爾摩沙。

是誰驅動著你？
　讓你無視洪水和降雪，
誰是那寄語相知者？
　讓你輕輕飛動
掠過無數個春光。

林明理攝影 / 圖

不，你是宙斯最精緻的巧思，
　如此難以接近，
無感於淚水與世間的悲涼，
那掠過的身影，卻使我心張望。

　　　　　　－2018/2/27

34.　Mountain butterflies

*Dr. Lin Ming-Li

Are you from a distant country
　Like me, carefree,
Drifting over ancient land, the mysterious valley,
From the rugged coast toward Formosa?

Who motivates you
　Making you ignore flood and snow?
Who is your bosom friend
　Making you fly gently
Through the splendour of spring?

No, you are Zeus's most exquisite ingenuity,
　So inaccessible
Unaffected by tears and sadness of the world,
Your fluttering silhouette pulls along my longing heart.

（Translator：Dr. William Marr）
－刊美國《亞特蘭大新聞》，2018/04/13，中英譯，
非馬譯，圖文。
－刊臺灣《秋水》詩刊，176 期，2018/07，頁 15。

35. 我倆相識絕非偶然

如首次展翅而飛的海鷗，
只想與你平行遨遊；
我會努力
絕不輕易墜落...
天空何其寬廣，為自由
我無懼黑暗和險惡，
只想沿著這路到潺潺水流。

－2018/03/24

Lin Mingli/painting

35.　It's no coincidence that we've met each other

*Dr. Lin Ming-Li

Like the　sea　dove　that flies for the first time,
It just wants to travel together with you;
I will　try hard
So that I'll never fall off easily...
How vast is the sky!　For freedom
I have no fear of darkness or danger.
I just want to follow this　path to the gurgling current.

（Translator Dr. William Marr）

－刊美國《亞特蘭大新聞》，
　2018/04/20，中英譯，非馬譯，圖文。

－刊臺灣《臺灣時報》，2018/04/11，
　圖文。

－刊臺灣（大海洋詩雜誌），第 98 期，
　2019/01，頁 19。

36. 致青山

我昂首
　如伸向天空的長頸鹿，
千朵萬朵雲兒掠過，
從綠油油的谷地到無邊的海角。
古老的土地上已沒有任何喧囂…
在這裡，
　時間靜止不動，
　月朦朧，鳥棲息。

－2018/03/17

Lin Mingli/painting

36. To the Green Mountain

*Dr. Lin Ming-Li

I   raise my head
   Like a giraffe stretches its neck toward the sky,
Thousands of clouds pass by,
From the green valley to the boundless cape.
There is no noise in this ancient land...
Here
   Time stands still,
   The moon is hazy, birds   are at rest .

（Translator：Dr. William Marr）

－刊臺灣《臺灣時報》，
2018/04/25，圖文。

－美國《亞特蘭大新聞》，
2018/08/03，中英詩，圖
文，非馬譯。

－刊臺灣《華文現代詩》，
第 19 期，2018/11，頁
72，油畫一幅。

－刊臺灣（大海洋詩雜誌），第 98 期，2019/01，頁 18。

37. 寒冬過後

在荒野的路途上，
周圍有渡鴨啼鳴
黎明姍姍來遲
但山風清涼。
一隻灰熊
饑餓地尋找食物，
麋鹿、狼群、美洲豹等
隱隱出沒。
當陽光照亮了
整個山脈，
啊，大自然的一切
就是一種純然的喜悅。

－2018/04/19

Lin Mingli/painting

37. After the winter

*Dr. Lin Ming-Li

In the wilderness,
There are ducks squawking around
The day dawns in a slow pace
And the mountain breeze is cool.
A hungry bear
Seeking for food,
Elks, wolves, leopards....
Making their vague appearance,
When the sun shines
On the entire mountain,
Ah, everything in nature
Is such a pure joy.

（Translator：Dr. William Marr）

－刊美國《亞特蘭大新聞》，
2018/04/27，中英譯，非馬譯，圖
文。
－刊臺灣《臺灣時報》，台灣文學版，
2018/11/14，水彩畫 1 幅。

38. 把和平帶回來

一切都很安靜
直到砲彈來襲
建築、作物和牲畜
　　被無情催毀
天空
　眼睜睜瞪著獨裁者的私慾
大地
　哭訴著侵略者的罪行
一隻白鴿
在黃昏中悲鳴
對著眼前無盡的道路
只有明月
用溫存的手撫慰著難民

－2018/03/29

Lin Mingli/painting

38.　Bring peace back

* Dr. Lin Ming-Li

Everything is quiet
Until the shells hit
The buildings, crops and livestocks
Ruthlessly destroy everything
The sky
Watches helplessly the dictator's lust
The earth
Weeps for the crime of the aggressors
A white pigeon
Cries in the dusk
Against the endless road ahead
Only the moon
Reassures the refugees with a tender hand

（Translator：Dr. William Marr）

－刊美國《亞特蘭大新聞》，2018/05/04，中英譯，非馬譯，圖文。

－刊臺灣《臺灣時報》，2018/10/24，圖文。

39. 當黎明時分

星月消隱碧空，
悅耳的鳥鳴和平野的風
混和著。陣陣稻香
在空氣中浮動；
我走上熟悉的路，
不再害怕會錯失什麼，
除卻你情真的信息，
充盈在彼此的眼中。

-2018/04/28

Lin Mingli/painting

39.　Stay with my heart

*Dr. Lin Ming-Li

The moon and stars disappeared from the blue sky,
The melodious songs of birds mixed with the breeze
Bursts of rice fragrance
Floating in the air;
I walked onto the familiar road,
No longer afraid of missing anything,
Except the messages of your true feeling
That fill our eyes.

（Translator：Dr. William Marr）

－刊美國《亞特蘭大新
　聞》，2018.05.1，中英
　譯，非馬譯，圖文。

－刊臺灣《臺灣時報》，
　2018.09.26，圖文。

40. 西子灣夕照

你的影像在
礁石浪潮中，
風甜甜地吹，
引我的思緒
留駐於心的記憶；
我記得
平灘上的每一足跡，
像今夜星辰般溫暖。
而我又告別了夕陽，
在大片天際線之下。
　　－2018/05/01

大海洋詩雜誌 － 18 －

林明理博士的詩(附英譯)

一、西子灣夕照
你的影像在
礁石浪潮中，
風甜甜地吹，
引我的思緒
留駐於心的記憶；
我記得
平灘上的每一足跡，
像今夜星辰般溫暖。
而我又告別了夕陽，
在大片天際線之下。

1. Sizihwan sunset
Your image is in the waves
　　among the reefs,
The wind blows sweetly
Leading my thoughts
To stay in the memory of my heart,
I remember
　　Every footprint on the beach,
Warm as the stars of tonight.
And I bid farewell to the setting sun again.
Under the vast skyline.

二、致青山
我昂首
宛如向天空的長頸鹿，
千朵萬朵雲翼飄過，
從綠油油的谷地到無邊的海角。
古老的土地上已沒有任何喧囂……
在這裡，
時間靜止不動，
月朦朧，鳥棲息。

2. To the Green Mountain
I raise my head
　　Like a giraffe stretches its neck toward the sky,
Thousands of clouds pass by,
From the green valley to the boundless cape.
There is no noise in this ancient land...
Here
Time stands still,
　　The moon is hazy, birds are at rest.

－ 19 － 大海洋詩雜誌

三、我倆相遇絕非偶然
好言天涯似我的碧海，
只想與你作伴同遊。
我會努力
還不夠藍還沉－
天空何其高遠，為自由！
沒有懼黑暗也敢望，
只想於著沿路到隱隱小徑。

3. It's no coincidence that we've met each other
Like the sea drove that ditch for the first time,
It just wants to travel together with you.
I will try hard
So that I'll never fall off easily...
How vast is the sky! For freedom,
I have no fear of darkness or danger,
I just want to follow this path to the gurgling cutting

四、長城
重、日日夜夜
從那條望遠處望去
彷聽無言的一切
看得到那一切
默然了的的敲詐手
都在那裡還在有朝的夜晚
歷非中、不再有聲響了

4. The Great Wall
Ire, day and night,
Looks from the tower through the mountain ridge line
Listens to
A heartwarming everything
The revisiting Honeysuckle
Whichare covered by the murmuring night shadows
And dreams, no longer feels say much

五、原野之聲
在雲中
或遊著眾神的腳步中
時而愉快
時而靜靜地穩
我從不期待奇蹟
也不感嘆在何如流
能誠實面對自己
是唯一的信念
你把唯唯之聲
就像原野之聲

5. Voice of the Wilderness
In the air
Or among the footsteps of the gods
Sometimes happy
Sometimes quietly vibrating
I never expect a miracle
Nor lament the passage of time
Being honest with myself
Working really hard
Is the only dependable thing
Just like the sound of this wilderness

40.　*Sizihwan sunset*

* Dr. Lin Ming-Li

Your image is in the waves
among the reefs,
The wind blows sweetly
Leading my thoughts
To stay in the memory of my heart;
I remember
Every footprint on the beach,
Warm as the stars of tonight.
And I bid farewell to the setting sun again,
Under the vast skyline.

（Translator：Dr. William Marr）

－刊臺灣《臺灣時報》，台灣文學版，
　2018/05/17，圖文。

－刊美國《亞特蘭大新聞》，2018/05/25，
　中英譯，非馬譯，圖文。

－刊大海洋詩刊 98 期 2019.01，林明理詩
　五首，西子灣夕照，致青山，我倆相
　絕非偶然，4.長城，5.原野之聲，非馬
　譯五詩 2

41. 雪啊雪

你知否？
一把鎖，
鎖了三代人，
鎖在這黃土地，
在風中，
編織
千百次夢想；
你知否？
每年風沙呼吼，
耕地貧瘠，
村民莫可奈何。
需什麼樣的奇蹟，
才能讓光明之路
繼續伸展？
需什麼樣的禱告，
才能讓這荒漠
逐步變成綠洲？
村民如此期望著——
雪啊雪，
在沙丘。
在土牆外，
我們織夢。

-2018/05/08.

41.　*Snow O snow*

* Dr. Lin Ming-Li

Do you know?
A latch,
Has Locked the people for three generations
In this yellow earth,
Woven thousands of dreams
　　In the wind.
Do you know?
Every year, the wind rustles
The poor farmland with ruthless sand,
The villagers have no other choice.
What kind of miracles are needed?
How can we make the way leading to light
Continue to stretch?
What kind of prayers do we need
To make this desert
An oasis?
The villagers are so looking forward to -
Snow O snow,
Over the dunes.
Outside the dirt walls,
We weave dreams.

（Translator：Dr. William Marr）

－刊美國《亞特蘭大新聞》，2018/05/25，
中英譯，非馬譯，圖文。

42. 路

一條無盡的路
橫臥在巨峰之間。
僅少數的村人，僧侶
沿著這路蜿蜒向前⋯

擁抱世界的夢想，
從青春的少年
到孤獨的暮年，
生命轉瞬即逝；

蒼天許我以歌——
像隻黑頭文鳥
在田野中自由飛翔，
領受大地賜給我的恩典。

--2018/04/16

42. The road

*Dr. Lin Ming-Li

An endless road
Lies between mountain peaks.
Only a few villagers and monks
Crawl   along this road...

The dream of embracing the world,
From the time of youth
To the lonely old age,
Life is fleeting;

Heaven gives me songs --
Like a blackbird
I fly freely among the fields,
Receiving the grace that the earth bestows upon me.

（Translator：Dr. William Marr）

－刊臺灣《笠詩刊》，325 期，2018/06，頁 81。
－刊美國《亞特蘭大新聞》，2018/05/25，中英譯，非馬譯，圖文。
－刊臺灣《臺灣時報》，2018/07/18，台灣文學版，圖文。

43. 重歸自然

這一片淺水海域
孕育出的野外天堂，
蝴蝶、小動物和鳥
充滿著多彩季節的旋律。

夏夜
以溫柔之風環繞島嶼，
外界紛紜和帶痛的思緒
似乎都離得很遠。

Lin Mingli/painting

只有圓月在林梢慢移，
而我的心
也在尋求重歸自然
——寧靜的聲音。

－2018/04/27

43.　*Return to nature*

* Lin Ming-Li

This wild paradise
bred in the shallow water area
Butterfly, small animals and birds
Full of colorful seasonal melody.

Summer night
When gentle winds embrace the island ,
Divisive and painful thoughts
Seem so far away.

Only the moon is slowly moving at the tip of the forest.
And my heart
tries to return to nature
——a quiet voice.

（Translator：Dr. William Marr）

－刊臺灣《臺灣時報》，
2018.05.23，圖文。

44. 老橡樹

經過五百年，
您的額頭刻滿了風霜
以及所有走過艱難的圖式；
任何歌咏
也不能描繪唱讚──
您手臂上沾附著滿滿露珠，
在晨光下閃耀，使我多麼震
動！
噢，上帝，
我飛翔的心……
獻上的不是浮誇，
而只是一首小小的詩歌，
猶如這夏夜的晚禱。

Lin Mingli/painting

* 來自欣賞攝影家 Thierry Kergroac'h
  的照片後，有感而思。
  －2018/05/23 寫於台灣。

44. An Old Oak

*Dr. Lin Ming-Li

After five hundred years,
Your forehead is covered with wind and frost
And traces of hardship;
No song
Can adequately praise you-
Your arms are covered with dew,
Shining in the morning light, and shocking me!
Oh God,
My heart is taking a flight...
My offering is not extravagant.
It's just a little poem,
A summer night's prayer.

* Inspired by the photo taken by Thierry Kergroac'h.
　－2018/05/23. Written in Taiwan.

（Translator：Dr. William Marr）

－刊臺灣《臺灣時報》，2018/06/06，圖文。
－刊美國《亞特蘭大新聞》，2018/06/01，非馬譯，圖文。

45. 夏日慵懶的午後

有座被鳥雀和
蓮花簇擁的小森林，
湖面似透鏡，
雲終於落下來。
我踮起腳尖，
按下快門的一瞬，
細碎的陽光是背景，
天空無語，卻令我沉迷。
我以為自己可以及時
找到真理和歡樂，
那遺世的孤獨
已離開很遠；
風總是靜靜地吹，
在這夏日慵懶的午後。

－2018/05/16

45.　The Lazy Summer Afternoon

*Dr. Lin Ming-Li

There was this little forest

Surrounded by birds and lotus flowers.

The cloud eventually fell

Upon the mirror-like lake.

I stood on tiptoe,

When I pressed the shutter of my camera,

With the fragmented sunlight as the back ground,

I was enthralled by the peaceful sky

And thought I could find truth and happiness in time,

While leave the loneliness of the world behind.

The wind blows gently

In this lazy summer afternoon.

（Translator：Dr. William Marr）
－刊美國《亞特蘭大新聞》，2018/06/01，非馬　譯，圖文。
－刊臺灣《華文現代詩》，第 18 期，2018/08，攝影 1 張，頁 75。
　　*2018/05/17 ERNESTO 於 12:49 PM
　　　Your poem, Mingli, is a perfumed fresh in summer
　　　Ernesto

46. 在那雲霧之間

萬物息息相連。
　峽谷郁郁青青，
座頭鯨乍現——
　隨 即沉入海底。
古老的石頭畫
把過去的歷史串連
　在天幕之間迴盪……
同樣的雨林，
從來由不得原住民選擇。
而那些盜伐者或狩獵者，
是否也該深思，
　動物將定居何處？

-2018/05/05.

Lin Mingli/painting

46. *Between the clouds*

*Dr. Lin Ming-Li

Everything is connected.
　The gorge is lush,
Humpback whales show up -
　Then sink to the bottom of the ocean.
Ancient stone paintings
Chain together past histories
　Reverberate in the sky...
The same rainforest,
Has never been chosen by many natives
And the timber stealers and hunters,
　Must　also consider
　Where should the animals live?

（Translator：Dr. William Marr）

－刊美國《亞特蘭大新聞》，2018/06/08，
　非馬　譯，圖文。

47. 如風往事

終究
一切都已結束
終究
讓愛遠颺
終究
獨自步上荊棘之路
我的靈魂懸在崖壁
　　　邊游邊躲

是誰
讓一切返回虛無
是誰
兀自矗立懸崖之後
不再夢寐以求什麼
愛，可以反覆難測
也可以歸於平淡……
　　　來去無蹤

－2018/05/30

47. Gone with the Wind

*Dr. Lin Ming-Li

Finally
Everything is over
Finally
Love flies　away
Finally
Alone on the thorny road
My soul is hanging over the cliff
　　Wandering and hiding

who is it
Letting everything return to nothingness
After climbing the cliff
No longer dreaming of love
Which can be　unfathomable
Or can be　insignificant......
　　Coming and going without a trace

（Translator：Dr. William Marr）

－刊美國《亞特蘭大新聞》，2018/06/08，中英譯，非馬譯。
－刊臺灣《秋水》詩刊，177 期，2018/10，頁 87，中英譯，
　非馬譯。

48. 原野之聲

在空中
或諸神的腳步中
時而愉悅
時而靜靜晃動

我從不期待奇蹟
也不感嘆歲月如流
能誠實面對自己
真正去努力
是唯一的信靠
恰如這原野之聲
使我安詳無憂

Lin Mingli/painting

－2018/05/13

48. Voice of the Wilderness

*Dr. Lin Ming-Li

In the air
Or among the footsteps of the gods
Sometimes happy
Sometimes quietly vibrating

I never expect a miracle
Nor lament the passage of time
Being honest with myself
Working really hard
Is the only dependable deed
Just like the sound of this wilderness
That makes me calm and peaceful

（Translator：Dr. William Marr）

－刊美國《亞特蘭大新聞》，2018/06/08，
　中英譯，非馬譯。
－刊臺灣《華文現代詩》季刊，第 18 期，
　2018/08，頁 75。
－刊臺灣《臺灣時報》，台灣文學版，
　2018/06/13，圖文。

49. 淡水紅毛城之歌

我總愛在深夜，開始傾聽。你在
冬天黎明的嘆息。
啊，寂寞的城。
你載著往日的歷史和明天的月光，
雙眼輕閉著，歌裡永遠縈繞著一條
母親的河；

*林明理博士

它總是那麼平靜——平靜地，
被風帶往大海的懷抱。
你就像詩曲，擁有一切的悲傷和歡樂。
你留在我眼底的雙眸，深邃而遺世。
露台的槍眼已成過眼雲煙，
故鄉的圓月永遠不會衰老；
然後，隱隱聽見，
觀音的微笑慢慢綻開，綿延成島嶼之花。
我聽見了草坪鏽砲上的歌聲，歌聲跳盪在

49. *Fortress San Domingo, Song of Danshui*

*Dr. Lin Ming-Li

I always love to, in the depth of night, start
listening. You are
Sighing at the dawn of winter.
Ah, lonely city.
You carry the history of yore and the moonlight of
tomorrow,
Two eyes gently closed, the song is forever
lingering with a motherly river;
It is always so quiet — quietly,
Carried away to bosom of the sea by wind.
You are like a poem, which is filled with all joys
and sorrows.
The eyes which you leave in my eyes are deep,
detached from the world.
The loophole on the terrace has been transient as a
fleeting cloud,
The hometown moon will never age;
Then, it is faintly hearable,
The smile of Kwan-yin slowly blossoms, spreading
into flowers on the island.
I have heard a song from the rusty artillery gun on
the turf, which is bouncing

冬天的童話裡，來回尋找失落的故事。

啊，我總愛在深夜，才開始傾聽；

你的歌聲——在流年的河裡，

隨著月輝的照耀，讓人感到溫暖而幸福。

In winter fairy tales, looking back and forth for lost stories.
Ah, I always love to, in the depth of night, start listening;
Your song — in the river of the running year,
With the shining of the moonlight, we feel warm and happy.

(Translator: Professor Zhang Zhizhong, Foreign Languages College, Tianjin Normal University)

譯者：現任天津師範大學外語系張智中教授

-

－刊美國《亞特蘭大新聞》，2018/06/15，中英譯，張智中教授英譯，圖文。

50. 大安溪夜色

溪谷傳來樂音，
鳥獸無言。
多美的母親之河！
果樹芬芳，
無所畏懼外界的一切。

再遠的故鄉，
我都看得見。
多美的瀑布，
多美的梯田。
多美的織作——祖靈之眼，
多美的紋面。

願我們部落與
另一端泰雅人，
都會永遠相伴相隨。
在山城，在溪畔，
啊，這歡愉的夜。

　　　　－2018/06/10.

　　註.泰雅人的織作中，最著名的祖靈之眼（Dowriq Utux Rudan），
是以兩個菱形所構成像似眼睛般的幾何圖形， 是代表泰雅人祖先對
族人的凝視。
　　　　－刊臺灣《臺灣時報》，2018/07/04，圖文。
　　　　－刊臺灣《秋水》詩刊，177 期，2018/10，頁 88。

50. Da-an River At　Night

*Dr. Lin Ming-Li

Music　comes　from　the valley
Birds and animals　remain　silent.
How beautiful is the mother river!
The fragrant fruit trees　are　not afraid of the world.

I can see　my　hometown
No　matter　how　far　away it　is.
So　beautiful is the waterfall,
So beautiful are the terraces.
So beautiful is the fabric - the eyes of the ancestors,
So　beautiful is its texture.

May our tribe and
The Atayal over the other side,
Always go hand in hand.
In the mountain city, beside the stream,
O,　what　a happy night.

Note. In Atayal 's fabric, the　famous ancestral eye　(Dowriq Utux Rudan) is a diamond-shape geometry, representing the gaze of the ancestors of the Atayal upon their descendants.

（Translator：Dr. William Marr）

－刊美國《亞特蘭大新聞》，2018/07/06，
中英譯，非馬英譯，圖文。

51. 七月的思念

在山丘盡頭的
　另一邊
無盡的海
岩岸的浪花
使我心悅。

藍色的風
　　掠過
漁舟點點
聽鳥啁啾
我輕閉著眼。

想念你
　如候鳥翩躚
而你是
大河展延
我唯一的思念。

-2018/06/29

51. July Longing

*Dr. Lin Ming-Li

Over the other side of the hill
　Is the boundless sea
The waves along the rocky shore
Make me happy.

Blue wind
Blows across
Fishing boats
While I listen to the voice of the
birds.
With slightly closed eyes.

I Miss you
　A migrating bird
And you
　Extending like a river
Become my only longing.

（Translator：Dr. William Marr）

　　－刊臺灣《人間福報》副刊，2018/07/12，
　　圖文。
　　－刊臺灣《臺灣時報》，2018/07/13，圖文。
　　－刊美國《亞特蘭大新聞》2018/08/03，
　　中英詩，林明理油畫，非馬譯。
　　－刊臺灣笠詩刊，第 326 期，2018/08，頁
　　84。

　　*2018/7 月 13 日 於 下午 7:14 法國名詩人 2019 年諾貝爾
獎候選人 Athanase Mail

　　So nice, dear Ming-Li. I fly this Sunday to
Bulgaria. There I will translate your poem !

　　Come back to Paris september 2.

　　Athanase

圖 45. 刊臺灣《臺灣時報》，
　　　 2018/07/13。

圖 45-2. 刊美國《亞大新
　　　　 聞》2018/08/03。

圖 45.-1 刊臺灣《人
　　　 間福報》副刊，
　　　 2018/07/12。

52. 平靜的湖面

在淡淡白色煙霧裡
你是思索中的詩人
看落葉褪盡
季節輪換的容貌

法文語譯

52. Un lac calme

*Dr. Lin Ming-Li

Au milieu du pâle brouillard,
Vous êtes le poète plongé dans des pensées profondes
Suivant du regard les feuilles qui s'évanouissent
Et la face de la nouvelle saison qui s'avance.

（Translated into French by Athanase Vantchev de Thracy）

52.　A Calm Lake

*Dr. Lin Ming-Li

In the pale fog
You are a poet in deep thought
Watching the leaves fading away
The changing face of a new season

←（此詩的法譯者，法國詩人阿薩納斯被提名為 2018 年諾貝爾獎的候選人。The poet's French translator, the French poet *Athanase Vantchev de Thracy* , was nominated for the 2018 Nobel Prize.）

—刊美國《亞特蘭大新聞》，中英法詩，2018/06/29，圖文

53 你的呼喚

— to 普希金 Aleksandr Pushkin
（1799-1837）

你的呼喚
能夠引起千萬個親切的懷念
眾神圍繞著你的步履
繁星垂掛在你的胸前
雪花輕輕唱
莫札特樂曲隱隱約約
我讀皇村的花園
紅梅花兒正開
如讀你不朽的詩篇

註.普希金鎮 沙皇村（Царское село）。

--2016.1.15

53.　Lorsque tu appelles

*Dr. Lin Ming-Li

À Alexandre Pouchkine (1799-1837)

Ta voix
Peut faire revivre mille souvenirs agréables.
Je sais que maintenant tu marches
En compagnie des dieux
Et que les étoiles brillent sur ta poitrine comme
des médailles.
Aujourd'hui, la neige chante doucement,
La musique de Mozart joue en arrière-plan
Et je lis des vers qui évoquent le jardin de Tsarskoïe Selo.
Les pruniers dans la cour qui annoncent le printemps
M'assurent que tes poèmes dureront toujours.

Note：

Tsarskoïe Selo: domaine ayant　appartenu　à la　famille impériale russe. Maintenant, il fait partie de la ville de Pouchkine et est classé au patrimoine mondial.

（Translator：Athanase Vantchev de Thracy）
－刊美國（亞特蘭大新聞），2018/03/23，中法譯。

54. 在愉悅夏夜的深邃處

從未忘記。
風雨摧蝕的
　　山海灣，
迎接耳語的浪花，
我們並肩跑往
　　遼闊的星野。

背後的風
古老漁村的想像——
　　恰如一個夢，
這路徑，錯落的腳印
　　和笑聲。

而今
在記憶中逐漸抹去的，
　　不是你逐浪的身影，
而是小小的思愁
　　隨波成藍色……
忽遠，又靠近了。

林明理　油畫

-2018/08/09

54. In the depth of a pleasant summer night *Lin Ming-Li

Never forget.
The weathered
　Mountain bay,
Greeting the whispering waves
We ran side by side
　On the vast starry field.

The wind behind us
The imagination of an ancient fishing village -
　Is like a dream,
This path, the footprints
　　And laughter.

Now
What is being gradually erased from my memory,
　Is not your shadow,
But a little longing
　Flowing with the blue waves...
Now it's far, now it's near.

（Translator：Dr. William Marr）

2018/8 月 9 日 Prof. Ernesto Kahan Mail to Ming-Li

Pleasant summer night to you, a beauty great poet girl.

一刊臺灣《人間福報》，副刊，2018/08/23，油畫一幅。
一刊臺灣《華文現代詩》，第 19 期，2018/11，頁 72，油畫一幅。
一中英詩刊美國《亞特蘭大新聞》，圖文，2018/08/31，油畫一幅。

55. 永安鹽田濕地

一條碎石小路
黃昏的堤岸
　　　無人走過
三五白鷺
　　　低低地
飛往泥灘

寂寞的鹽田啊
　　更遠處
還有高高
踮起腳尖的水鳥
夜鷺在風中
　　　嘎嘎啼叫

是的，這一帶
曾是候鳥的天堂
而我所企盼的
　　恰如這清風
從紅樹林傳來的
鳥聲越來越近
　　月在水上

Lin Mingli/painting

55.　The Yongan Wetland

*Dr.Lin Ming-Li

A gravel path
Embankment at dusk
　　No one passing by
Except a few   egrets
　　　Flying low
Toward the mud   field

　Farther away
　　From the lonely salt pan
Some waterfowls are standing   tall   on their tiptoes
Night herons in the wind
　　　Are howling

Yes, this area
Used to be a paradise for migratory birds
And what I am hoping for   right now
　　Is just like this breeze
From the mangroves
The sounds of birds are getting closer
　　The moon on the water

　　*高雄永安濕地曾是台南以南最大的鹽灘濕地，兼具鹽業文化歷史、紅樹林生態及珍貴遷移性鳥類資源，而今需相關單位有效管理，以利生態永續發展。　　－2018.8.21

　　*我將此詩 Mail 給 Ernesto 並祝福他即將在 2018 年 10 月應邀到中國參加世界詩人大會。Prof. Ernesto Kahan 在 2018 年 8 月 24 日 mail to Ming-Li，令我開懷。

　　－刊臺灣《臺灣時報》副刊，2018/09/05，圖文。
　　－中英詩刊美國《亞特蘭大新聞》，2018/09/28，圖文，非馬譯。
　　－中英詩，台灣《秋水詩刊》，178 期，2019.01，頁 91，非馬譯。

（Translator：Dr. Willian Marr）

*As the largest salt wetland south of Tainan, the Yongan Wetland in Kaohsiung possesses the history of salt industry , mangrove ecology and precious migratory bird resources. Now it needs effective management to sustain the continued development of the ecology. -2018.8.21

* I will mail this poem to Ernesto and wish him that he will be invited to China to attend the World Poet Conference in October 2018. Prof. Ernesto Kahan mailed to Ming-Li on August 24, 2018, which made me happy.

I wanted to meet you in China
You are a beautiful poet and painter
I hope you are smiling all the time
Ernesto

56. Love is…

Love is
交會的眼神
　驚喜的一瞬
沒有虛飾
　彷若重生
沒有謊言
　只有真誠
它是自由的風
　不羈而難覓
哪怕是寸步千里
或千山萬水
無須承諾
沒有怨尤
Love is near you
在心的最深處

－2018/08/28

56.   Love is...

*Dr. Lin Ming-Li

Love is
The moment of surprise
   when the eyes meet
No frills
   Like in a rebirth
No lies
   Only sincerity
It is the wind of freedom
   Carefree yet hard to find
Either a few steps
Or thousands of miles
There is no commitment
Nor complaints
Love is near you
From the depth of my heart

（Translator：Dr. William Marr）

－中英詩刊美國（亞特蘭大新聞），
2018/09/21，圖文，非馬譯。

57. 向 G＋BTP 致謝

秋日的光，池畔的花影
　三五隻逗留的蜜蜂，
卻讓我常在此流連。
感謝 G＋，
讓我喜愛攝影的念頭出現，
又召喚我共享
　花卉特色系列的園地，
讓我歡慰、感恩和雀躍。
我願坐上星夜的橋畔，
　像一朵堅強的花，
溫存地伸向無垠的天空，
為大地而歌，並努力成長！

攝影作品（Purple water lily,
its flower language: dreamy,
pure, good luck）：林明理

註.2018.10.16 收到 Google＋BTP PRO FLOWER FEATURED
COLLECTION

　　通知我在網站貼的攝影照片被收錄在「花卉特色系列」，
和「PRO Winners WBP Oct.14-20，2018」，倍感榮幸，在此向攝
影家 Heinfried Kuthe 及 BTP 致謝。
https://plus.google.com/+BesttopphotographerFlowerPRO
https://plus.google.com/+PROWinners

57.　Thanks to G＋BTP

*Dr. Lin Ming-Li

The light of autumn, flowery shadows by the pool
　　Three or five lingering bees,
Often draw me here.
Thanks to G＋,
Which solicits my love for photography,
And calls me to enjoy
　　A gardenful of fair flowers,
And I'm filled with comfort and joviality.
I'd like to stand on the bridge of a starry night,
　　Like a strong-willed flower,
Which tenderly stretches heavenward,
　　While growing and singing for the earth.

Note: On October 16, I received a notice from Google＋BTP PRO FLOWER FEATURED COLLECTION, telling me that my photos at the network station have been collected into "Series of Flowers" and "PRO Winners WBP Oct.14-20, 2018", which is a great honor. Hence my thanks to photographer Heinfried Kuthe and BTP!

　　https://plus.google.com/+BesttopphotographerFlowerPRO

（天津師範大學張智中教授英譯，Translated by Professor Zhang Zhizhong of Tianjin Normal University）

57. My Thanks to G+BTP

*Dr. Lin Ming-Li

Autumnal light, in the shadow of flowers
Three or five bees linger at the poolside ,
Attracting me to hang around here.
Thanks   to G+,
Arousing my love of photography,
Calling me to share the joy
Of the garden of floral featured series,
I am so grateful and excited.
I would like to sit on the bridge in the starry night.
Like a flower,
Reaching for the vast sky,
Working hard to bloom and sing for the earth.

Note   .2018.10.16   Received   Google+BTP   PRO   FLOWER FEATURED COLLECTION

I am grateful to Photographers Heinfried Kuthe and BTP that the photos posted on my website were included in the "Floral Featured Series" and "PRO Winners WBP Oct.14-20, 2018". (Translator：Dr. William Marr)

-中英譯刊美國《亞特蘭大新聞》，2018/10/19，攝影作品1 張。

http://www.atlantachinesenews.com/News/2018/10/10-19/B_ATL
_P08.pdf

PRO Winners

2018 年 10 月 22 日, 下午 3:16

Time to announce our **WBP Winners** from last week's **Featured Collections selected by our editors from our BTP Pro Pages.** Another great collection of some of the most outstanding photography by amazing photographers!
Thanks to our amazing team for all their hard work. Please be sure to update your tags. Interested in having a chance to be here? Please read and be sure to use to correct tags so we do not miss your work.
bit.ly/proproject
(Pro Pages Team)
*Our beautiful cover photo comes from: +Sergey Stratov
Congratulations go to:
+博士林明理

https://plus.google.com/collection/sWVbeE
Pro Winners WBP Oct 14-20 2018

58. 秋雨，總是靜靜地下著...

十月最後的一抹暮色
一切都是那麼寧靜
一隻黑鳥悄悄靠近
　　又悄悄離開
哦　朋友
　　我沒有忘記
　　又怎能忘記......
我似鼓翼的蛾
　　努力向前
　　永不墜落
也許，你也在夜雨中
　　等待雲霧散開
讓我想像
　　在遙遠的過去
我們曾經一起
　　走入光芒裡
你的輕言細語
　讓我滿耳充滿幸福

林明理畫圖

-2018.10.20

58. Autumn rain, always quietly falling... *Dr.Lin Ming-Li

The last twilight of October
   All is so tranquil
Only one black bird quietly approaches
   Then quietly leaves
O friend
   I have not forgotten
   How can I forget...
Like a flying moth
   I strive to move on
   Never fall
Maybe you are also in the night rain at this moment
   Waiting for the clouds and fog to clear
Let me imagine
   In the distant past
We were together
Your happy whispers
   Fill my ears

（Translator：Dr. William Marr）

－刊臺灣《臺灣時報》，2018/10/31，圖文。

*2018 年 10 月 30 日 Prof. Ernest o Kahan Mail to Ming-Li
Your poem is superb   Love you

59. 給我的朋友——Heinfried Küthe

我感謝你。

在晚秋一個多雲的黃昏，

朋友，

那令人愉悅的蓮花，

豆娘，蜜蜂，啁啾的鳥聲，

　　不久便一一離開。

移開我的視線，拍下的

那一瞬，

您鼓勵的語言變成了

　　永恆的喜樂。

林明理攝影作品
(red lotus and damselfly)

　　*2018 年 10 月 23 日，獲得 Google＋BTP 「PRO FLOWER FEATURED COLLECTION」通知「It's my pleasure to add your excellent photo to our PRO FLOWER FEATURED COLLECTION．Be sure to follow our wonderful collections to see many great photos including yours.Have a wonderful day!(Heinfried Küthe)，特此致謝。

－2018.10.29

https://plus.google.com/+BesttopphotographerFlowerPRO/posts/RF2nCnFzH9B

59. To my friend, Heinfried Küthe

*Dr.Lin Ming-Li

I thank you,
My friend.
In a cloudy evening of late autumn,
Before the pleasant lotus,
Damselflies, bees, and chirping birds,
　disappeared one after another,
I took this picture.
At that moment,
I heard the arrival of your encouraging words
　What a joy!

*On October 23, 2018, I received a letter from Heinfried Küthe of PRO, informing me that my photo was added to their PRO FLOWER FEATURED COLLECTION. What a joy!
（Translator：Dr. William Marr）

　－中英譯刊美國《亞特蘭大新聞》，
2018.11.02，攝影作品1張，非馬譯。

60. 修路工人

幾個工人，揮汗如雨，
　小心修補長長的路——
開車的，揮旗的，發號施令的，
　還有一隻小黃狗，
各盡其責，緊密相依。
　只有天空注視著這一切。
一場驟雨，來得太急，
被無端撞飛的小夥子
　血流不止，斷了氣。
是的，天空的雲彩依舊，
施工繼續進行，
　含著淚，修補著最後一段路。

林明理/作畫

啊命運之神，你不可能不關注
　這些底層勞動者，
也不可能不回答他們的狂喜和悲痛。
是的，哪怕人生短暫如滄海一粟，
黑暗終究無法隱蔽黎明的曙光。
當朝陽的浪濤，又輕輕地拍擊……
　海鷗振翅騰起
　沒時間哭泣。　　　－2018.11.3

－刊美國（亞特蘭大新聞），2018/11/16，圖文，中英譯，非馬譯。
－刊臺灣（臺灣時報），2018/11/28，圖文。
－刊笠詩刊，328期，2018.12.頁105。

60. Construction Workers

*Dr. Lin Ming-Li

Several workers, sweating,
　Carefully repaired the long road—
Driving, waving, giving signals,
　Among them was a little yellow dog,
All worked as a team,
　Under the watchful eye of the sky.
In the middle of a sudden shower
A young man was accidentally hit by a truck
　And bled to death.
The sun behind the clouds kept rising,
The construction continued to move forward.
With tears, they repaired the last section of the road.
Ah, god of destiny, how could you watch without paying any attention
　To these workers,
It is also impossible not to answer to their ecstasy and grief.
Yes, even if life is as tiny as a grain in the sea,
After all, darkness cannot hide the morning light.
When the waves of the sunlight gently
　Slap..The seagulls open their wings。
　No time to cry

（Translator：Dr. William Marr）

61. 大雪山風景

當夕陽將盡
　層層雲海
從淡紫變成緋紅
　飄滿天際。
一隻松鴉飛起，
　點亮村舍的燈火。
在大雪山
　林海的初冬之中，
我夢見了冬螢飛舞，
　飛鼠鳴唱。
風和月兒攜手散步，
山羌豎起耳朵——
　傾聽我的詩思。
夜是朦朧的，
星際的樹梢…
　越黑越閃亮。
思念無邊，恰如
部落的歌聲　緩緩
　流瀉而來。

林明理/作畫

－2018.11.16

註：大雪山位於台灣苗栗縣泰安鄉與台中市和平區交界
處，為台灣的名山。

－刊臺灣（臺灣時報），2018/12/19，圖文。

61. Daxue Mountain scenery

*Dr.Lin Ming-Li

Right before sunset
　　Layers of clouds
From pale purple to blush
　　Fill up the sky.
A jay flies up,
　　to light the lights in the cottage.
In the Daxue mountain
　　In the early winter of Lin Hai,
I dream of the dancing winter fireflies ,
　　And the singing flying rats.
The wind and the moon walk together,
Hawthorns raise their ears -
　　To listen to my poems.
The night is hazy,
Interstellar treetops...
　　the darker the more shiny.
The boundless longing
Like the song of the tribe
　　Flow slowly　towards me.

　　Note. Daxue Mountain, a famous mountain in Taiwan, is located at the junction of Taian Township, Miaoli County, and Heping District, Taichung City.-2018.11.16

（Translator：Dr. William Marr）

－刊美國（亞特蘭大新聞）圖文，2018/12/14，中英譯，非馬譯。

62. 你的榮光

——給 prof. Ernesto Kahan

我敬佩你，朋友，
和平的使者
悲憫的心胸。
聖潔的目光
比藍天還清澄，
深深浸潤著學子心田，
也不可分地貫穿在
愛與和諧之中。

　　*這是 2018 年 11 月的印度獎，該獎項是印度兩所大學的榮譽博士，以表彰 prof. Ernesto Kahan 對全球和平、愛與和諧的奉獻精神。

－2019/1/3

photo：Ernesto Kahan won the award

62. *Your glory*

— to prof. Ernesto Kahan

*Dr. Lin Ming-Li

I admire you, friend,

The messenger of peace

With a compassionate heart.

Your holy eyes

Are more luminous than the blue sky,

Penetrating the hearts of the students,

Through
Love and harmony.

* Prof. Ernesto Kahan was awarded,in November of 2018, an honorable doctorate degree by two universities in India for his dedication to world peace, love and harmony.（Translator：Dr. William Marr）

－刊美國（亞特蘭大新聞），2019/01/11。

photo：Ernesto Kahan won the award

你的榮光
—— 給 prof. Ernesto Kahan

*林明理博士

我敬佩你，朋友，
和平的使者
悲憫的心胸。
聖潔的目光
比藍天還清澄，
深深浸潤著學子心田，
也不可分地貫穿在
愛與和諧之中。

＊這是 2018 年 11 月的印度獎，該獎項是印度兩
所大學的榮譽博士，以表彰 prof. Ernesto Kahan
對全球和平、愛與和諧的奉獻精神~~2019/1/3

Your glory
— to prof. Ernesto Kahan
*Dr. Lin Ming-Li

I admire you, friend,
The messenger of peace
With a compassionate heart.
Your holy eyes
Are more luminous than the blue sky,
Penetrating the hearts of the students,
Through
Love and harmony.
* Prof. Ernesto Kahan was awarded, in
November of 2018, an honorable doctorate
degree by two universities in India for his
dedication to world peace, love and harmony.
(Translator：Dr. William Marr)

www. AtlantaChineseNews.com P.O. B

2019.1.11

二、已刊登的詩作（尚未翻譯區）

Published poems (not yet translated)

1. 寫給屈原之歌

今夜，我在汨羅歌唱
用我粗獷的語言和深情
你的眼神加注了
真實節奏
在風中，彷彿江水
投射出高貴的氣質

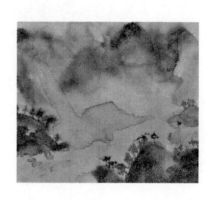

而我的歌不說你的傷心
只順著江畔奔跑
星海曉得
你的才華豐盈深厚
流浪心靈中
完成了中國不朽的辭賦

我看見歲月流逝
也聆聽出你歌裡的
沉默與堅韌
你擎起一盞燈

照亮了
人類絕世的光芒

今夜，我在汨羅歌唱
屈原
這名字迴盪著我
你的詩園是我四季的庇護所
而留給我們的詩句
如迎向曙光的百合

－刊在美國《亞特蘭大新聞》，2018/01/12.

2. 臨夏頌

1.我在天空寫下你
　　松鳴飛瀑的名字
　安坐在南無台和玉皇峰交界處
　那清澈、悅耳的音樂
　重覆著歡快的音節
　　一遍遍…
　那是最奪目的美。
　太陽出來時
　濺起的細珠，如煙似霧
　　把我的思想擱淺了
　而你是詩人的門生
　滿眼是樂園
　　──松鳴岩
　　天堂般完美
　　如王維的詩歌。

2.這翠色的原始森林
　　已歷經無數風霜的考驗，

連挺拔的擎天柱也動容。秋季
使我樂於想像
以一種海燕的姿勢
　　輕輕挪移，悠遊其中
或泊在千里之外，聽你向我招喚
　　聲聲如星海。
當思想脫離天地的糾葛，而你
　　成為風的使者：引我
在你的磅礴之氣的懷抱裡，
有如根枝相擁的連理松在閃耀。
當萬物齊聲歡頌──
我願在星月中
　　與你遨遊。

　　　－刊在美國《亞特蘭大新聞》，2018/01/12。

3. 在我窗前起舞

和風歇在桂花樹梢
窗外滿是絨毯兒
每一片
都似柳絮的輕柔

當黃昏的淡雲飄來
你便在我的眼底隱逝了...... 那時
冬原正是一片空曠，將慢慢，更慢地
透出明亮嚴肅的冷光——

－2018/01/05

－刊在美國《亞特蘭大新聞》，
2018/01/12.

4. 亞城雪景

隔著窗紗，我想像雪地上空
有隻山鷹掠過森林；
我聽見亞城的呼喚
和大雁的嘎嘎聲。

路盡處，狐狸緊挨著
野兔的腳印，快速
追趕過去，像樹鳥兒
穿過松林中。

*美國亞特蘭大的雪景 /
LUCY 攝影

而妳對我邊揮手，邊微笑，
那一望無際的林海
與遠方朦朧的城鎮，
或在意味著耶誕在即的等候？

　*今晨，美國作家藍晶電郵一張多年前自拍於亞城窗外雪景的照片，有感而詩。-2017.11.22

　－刊美國《亞特蘭大新聞》，2017/11/24，圖文。

5. 早　櫻

掠過花溪的櫻之影
波光瀲漾的山之音
周圍在歡唱，在漫舞，
而我感到幸福的是
那微雨中慢坡的小路，
那影樹交錯中的粉紅
──像個花仙子
　　在香階的霧中……

林明理/作畫

－2017/11/24 感恩節

－刊臺灣《臺灣時報》，2017/12/13，圖文。
－刊美國《亞特蘭大新聞》，2018/01/05，圖文。

6. 永懷文學大師──余光中

您是永恆的詩人
時時夢繫故國和
　福爾摩沙的美好
今夜，星子為你讚美吟咏
歌聲裡的芬芳
　在風中悠揚
　在紅紅的耶誕花上
　　發著光

林明理/作畫

－2017.12.14 同悼（著名詩人余
光中教授逝世於 2017 年 12 月
14 日，享壽 90 歲。

－刊美國《亞特蘭大新聞》，
　2017/12/22，圖文。

－刊臺灣《秋水》詩刊，175，
　2018/04，頁 52。

7. 寫給麗水的歌

八百里甌江，流過
大陸最美的麗水
流過縱衡交錯的林海，
流過古剎旁的飛瀑，
絕壁被煙雨和彩虹繚繞，
是青碧如藍的
草甸，馬尾松，
黑麂和涓涓小溪
長傍的所在，盈著飄零的
野花，噢，綠谷的戀人。

一個沉睡的古村落
數聲雞鳴，喚醒了安靜的夢幻
——畬鄉山歌在夢裡，
夢裡的朝陽
爬上黃泥的老牆、石子路
有村民說笑著，
擔子裡，筍尖、香蘑和溪魚，

這些記憶裡的花香
飄舞的畬族彩帶，
又在我心中澎湃不已；

彷彿，我已然回去了
我的額上被輕輕一吻
來自於畬族熱情的鼻息。
是的，那青瓷、寶劍和石雕的
印跡，是獻給歷史的宏偉之作
而村民的歌聲啊，
深化那一片莽莽青山
包容一切的林相萬物
延續在紅塵的陽光中迴盪…
迴盪在麗江的空氣中。

　　　－2017/11/15 寫於台東市午後
　　　－刊臺灣《大海洋詩雜誌》，LARGE OCEAN POETRY
　　　　QUARTERLY.第 97 期，2018.07，頁 86.
　　　－此詩獲浙江省麗水市「秀山麗水，詩韻處州」地名詩歌大賽
　　　　三等獎，臺灣林明理詩（寫給麗水的歌）。

　　　2017.12

　　.http://www.360doc.com/content/17/1215/12/41690297_71328455
　　　7.shtml

8. 我將前往美麗的松蘭山

秋葉已經凋零
北風在海峽中瑟瑟喧囂，
十一月
星空萬里無垠，
我將前往美麗的松蘭山
在海灣上聽浪擊岩壁，
彌陀古寺裡，——梵音
　　柔和而細膩
　　　　在寂靜的空氣中。

我將看著陽光
　　在灘面上閃爍，
海鳥向熟睡的島礁
　　歡欣地唱和著。
當金色的千米長沙
　　兵寨等等遺跡
　　　…浮上眼前…
我聽到遙遠的聲音，

聲音來自這碧水相擁的
小小半島，
卻成了我思念的方向。

啊　我祈禱
行於象山半島的旅人
往山川洞穴尋幽的人
往石浦老街坊走的人
都邁著愉快的步伐
　　　在這山海之下
　　　讓地球不停轉啊轉
而我的心伴著帆影和燈舞
輕輕滑過那山麓和沙灣。

　　　　　　--2017/11/28 寫於台灣
-刊美國《亞特蘭大新聞》，2017/12/29。

9. 時光裡的比西里岸

真希望自己是那奔流不息的大海中的一朵浪花。

我穿過比西里岸一條小巷出來。

最美的風景，總是要在自己心裡喚起的感動之下才存在，

那些潮聲與霧雨來臨前的八拱跨海步道橋……

像是美麗的邂逅，抑或夢中————

—2017/12/01 寫於台東

林明理攝影作品地點：三仙台。台東（三仙台原名「比西里岸」（阿美族語：Pisilisn 意為養羊之地）

—刊美國《亞特蘭大新聞》，2017/12/29，圖文。

—刊臺灣《臺灣時報》，台灣文學版，2018/08/01，圖文。

10. 給我最好的朋友一個*聖誕* 祝福

在這繽紛的佳節
無論你身處之處下雪
　　或者不會下雪
當月光輕灑在藍海上
啊朋友
你聽見了嗎
我將祈願變成千隻雪鳥
　　飛向你──
恰午夜時分的耶誕神曲
　　滿耳都是祝福

林明理/作畫

－2017/12/24

－刊美國《亞特蘭大新
聞》，2018/01/05，圖
文。

11. 淡水紅毛城之歌

我總愛在深夜，開始傾聽。你在
冬天黎明的嘆息，聲音彷彿呢喃一般。
啊，寂寞的城。
你載著往日的歷史和明天的月光，
雙眼輕閉著，歌裡永遠縈繞著一條母親的河；
它總是那麼平靜——平靜地，
被風帶往大海的懷抱。
你就像詩曲，擁有一切的悲傷和歡樂。
你留在我眼底的雙眸，深邃而遺世。
就像數百年前的月光，輕輕
繞過你肩膀……風笛在行進。
露台的槍眼已成過眼雲煙，
故鄉的圓月永遠不會衰老；
而我愛在古城的中心，在空蕩蕩船艙的
碼頭旁，踱來踱去。
這裡，時間緩慢到我幾乎察覺不到細雨在飛，
如雪般精緻排列。然後，隱隱聽見，
觀音的微笑慢慢綻開，綿延成島嶼之花。

我聽見了草坪鏽砲上的歌聲，歌聲跳盪在

冬天的童話裡，來回尋找失落的故事。

啊，我總愛在深夜，才開始傾聽；

你的歌聲——在流年的河裡，

隨著月輝的照耀，讓人感到溫暖而幸福。

*淡水紅毛城被視為台灣現存最古老的建築之一，前方置有四尊嘉慶十八年製成的古砲；前英國領事官邸在主堡東側，為兩層式紅磚洋樓，迴廊立面呈半圓拱型，欄杆則由綠色釉瓶組成，為著名景點之一。

－2017.11.9.

　　－刊台灣《笠詩刊》LI POETRY，324 期，2018/04，頁 54.

　　－刊美國《亞特蘭大新聞》，2018/01/05，圖文。

http://www.atlantachinesenews.com/News/2018/01/01-05/B_ATL_P08.pdf

林明理博士於淡水紅毛城

12. 寫給鞏義之歌

1.致鞏義市

在遠方溫婉的春雨
和夢寐在你的光亮之中
我將串起的驚嘆
變成輕輕滑進海峽的小槳
直奔開拓紀念杜甫的故鄉，
在那裡，有百家的碑林
與寬闊的詩香
那清澈、悅耳的森林之歌
重覆著歡快的音節
一遍遍：
松柏，眾鳥，流泉——
在那裡，美是最奪目的。
而你
永遠在前進的風雨中
迎向光明的世界
你比想像更美好
你比春花更繁茂！

2.石居部落

我愛這古樸的村莊
一片片山高林密
湖泊也像一首小詩那樣歌著

——我看見
祖先的窯洞
沉浸在這靜謐的星夜裡；
這是河洛文化的發祥地
革命軍老區也曾在此住紮
這是遊子寄託鄉愁之地
連古老的馬燈
都訴説著和我一樣懇切的話。

3.告別杜甫

我用天空寫下你的名字
你沿著足徑
在地圖上飛行
數千年過去了
在千里沃野的天際之下
你的思想和濟世情懷
仍影響著歷史
你的歌也體現了現實，
你的額上刻上了雨露和
溫暖明亮的光線
從老城的舊居
撼動著宇宙和神州；
而我在細雨中
以一種海燕之姿
輕輕...越過海域，
聽祖國聲聲招喚

相思如飛雪。

－刊美國《亞特蘭大新聞》，2018/05/04。

13. 民視「飛閱文學地景」 節目錄影紀實

*林明理博士（Dr. Lin Ming-Li）

　　2018 年 6 月 25 日，我愉快地步入台北市濟南路的「齊東詩舍」，應邀於民視（FORMOSA TELEVISION）「飛閱文學地景」的訪談與錄影製作。在此特別感謝導演涂文權、攝影師杜星助、執行製作石宛蓉、同仁王雅楨、邱宣穎及燈光師、梳妝師等製作小組的協助，得以順利完成錄影。附錄現場吟詩的全文如下：

淡水紅毛城之歌 (節錄)　*林明理

我總愛在深夜，
開始傾聽。
你在
冬天黎明的嘆息，

啊，寂寞的城。
你載著往日的歷史和明天的月光，
雙眼輕閉著，
歌裡永遠縈繞著一條母親的河；
它總是那麼平靜——平靜地，
被風帶往大海的懷抱。

輕輕
繞過你肩膀⋯⋯
風笛在行進。
露台的槍眼已成過眼雲煙，
故鄉的圓月永遠不會衰老；

這裡，
時間緩慢到我幾乎察覺不到細雨在飛，
如雪般精緻排列。

你的歌聲——在流年的河裡，
隨著月輝的照耀，
讓人感到溫暖而幸福。

　　接著，由涂導演親自提問有關此詩創作的過程。訪談內容大致是這樣的：

　　我推介的地景，是新北市淡水鎮的古蹟**紅毛城**（閩南語：Âng-mn̂g-siâⁿ）。它前後歷經西班牙、荷蘭、明、清代以及英國等不同使用者整修。*紅毛城的九面旗幟代表著它三百餘年來的歷史演變過程*。我第一次看到淡水紅毛城時，感覺它像是在訴說著時代的轉變。我期待將此詩記錄下來它的影像並與歷史記憶有所連結。如今，這座紅毛城已回到我們台灣政府所管轄。我從這座老城的二樓美麗的綠釉花瓶欄杆前，遙想當年曾有的戰事，如今這些前塵舊事已成過眼雲煙，耳邊也聽不到槍林炮火之聲。只有一輪千古不變的圓月，還是俯視著福爾摩沙，還是俯視著母親之河，俯視著這座三百多年來歷史的老城。只有母親之河－淡水河與這座老城唇齒相依。它的目光隨著這條母親之河，平緩地流向大海，它的視線也越看越遠了。

　　我想，淡水紅毛城留給我們這一代最珍貴的，不只是它是全台灣最古老建築之一，也不只它是重要的古蹟，而是每次我們回首看到它的身影，傾聽到它的歌聲以及背後的歷史故事時，我們就會更加熟悉我們台灣的歷史，也就會體會到我們這一代在寶島台灣的自由土地上，是幸福的。

　　錄影結束前，我也用一句話來介紹「飛閱文學地景」節目。我感性地說：「我是林明理，全新的「飛閱文學地景」，讓你看見台灣之美，使人倍感親切！」並記錄了我手寫此詩的影像。等大家一起拍攝幾張大合照，已近下午四點，離情依依。然後，我又坐上普悠瑪火車，結束這第四次民視節目錄影的難忘之旅。

　　　　　　　　　　　　　　　－2018/6/26晚上，寫於台東。

照片 1.民視「飛閱文學地景」執行製作石宛蓉等工作團隊與林
　　　明理老師於 2018 年 6 月 25 日採訪錄影後合照。
照片 2.林明理老師和涂文權導演錄影後合照於台北市「齊東詩
　　　舍」。
照片 3.林明理詩作「淡水紅毛城之歌」錄影後，與製作組大合
　　　照。
照片 4..照片 5.民視 FTV【飛閱文學地景】，執行製作石宛蓉攝
　　　影於「齊東詩舍」。

—刊美國《亞特蘭大新聞》，2018/06/29，合照 3 張。

　　*1.獲 2019 年諾貝爾候選人的法國詩人 Athanase Vantchey de Thracy

　　於 2018.6 月 26 日 於 下午 3:32 MAIL

I am so happy for you, my dear excellent Poet Ming-Li !!! Athanase

*2.美國詩人非馬(馬為義博士)於 2018.年 6 月 26 日 於 下午 5:46MAIL

高興看到妳大豐收
祝福
非馬

*3.義大利名詩人 Giovanni **G. Campisi**2018/6/26 MAIL
Hi Ming-Li，
美麗的照片 。
我看到你的朋友很多。
恭喜！他們很棒。
我發給你我寫的這首詩。
Un abbraccio.
约翰月 26 日 於 下午 8:54
Ciao Ming-Li,

bellissime le tue foto.
Ho visto che ci sono tanti tuoi amici.
Complimenti! Sono meravigliosi.
Ti mando questa poesia che ho appena scritto.
Un abbraccio.
Giovanni

*4.Prof. Ernesto Kanan Mail to Lin Ming-Li 祝賀我第二十本新書《現代詩賞析 Appreciation of the work of Modern Poets》出版於 2018/06，台北市文史哲出版社。

2018/06/18，ERNESTO 於 12:14 AM MAIL

Congratulations my poet for this new achievement. In the future new generations will mention you as for your superb poetry
love, Ernesto

14. 冬 望

梨花底
容顏是一朵青空的飛雲
水珠在臉上
破曉在一方

初醒後
那蘋果也似的雙頰
充滿天真清脆的笑聲
飄揚迴響
掠過山巔水色

我刻不出這圖騰
後有淺澗
前有石級
一幅冰綃
而開展的宮闕

將茶裡的醇香
吟味與枝頭的精靈⋯⋯

　　－刊於臺灣《人間福報》，副刊，2009/02/02。

15. 從海邊回來

悠悠淡淡，晚歸的星
溜上冬青樹，風
拎著裙襬，沿著槐花巷
從黃牆的寺院跑回
隨鐘鼓，輕輕一敲
簷滴聲
不斷

幾隻舢舨，白濤閃耀
碎在浪峰的盡頭
在那被吹得彎彎的
平灘上，看見自己
影子的延展
伸到蒼海
又落在腳前

紅燈點點，葉灑石階
我是羞藏在夜露裡的綠草
告訴我
那八萬四千的詩偈
隨風低吟
是否也淌進遊子的心田
燃起另一種慈悲

—刊於臺灣《人間福報》，副刊，2009/7/3。

16.鹿野高台之歌

我的目光凝視著。
當熱氣球冉冉升起，
就像夏夜裡飛舞的
螢光，點綴著天空。

八月已經來臨，
山巒一片綠意，
在流水的音樂聲中，
白雲在輕輕歡唱。

林明理 2018/07 油畫作品

那是一隻白鷺，
飛過田野和溪流，
飛過都蘭山和縱谷，
飛進了睡鄉。

啊，讓我做一輪明月，
做你的回憶，
做你永遠的等待，

做你擦身而過的星子。

就像這清晨。
我們每年相約的日子，
這喜悅湧上鹿野高台，
永遠不躲不藏。

—2018.7.29
—刊臺灣《臺灣時報》，2018/08/015.
—刊美國《亞特蘭大新聞》，2018/08/17.

17. 六十石山小夜曲

每年的八至九月間，我總想乘幾朵白雲，順著花東縱谷的周邊延伸，經歷了碧海波濤和壯闊山脈間的翱翔，最後都會停泊在六十石山前。

那綠色的山巒斜坡，無以數計的是一片澄黃的花海。

清晨時分，雲嵐繚繞，花木還滿綴著露珠。即使不是盛放的季節，悅耳的風聲，綿延壯麗的田畝，總是如波浪般層層推進。

林明理 /2018/07 油畫作品

山俯瞰著廣達三百公頃的金針田，風依然輕微地掠過我小小的心舟，泛成音符……那舞動的旋律，隨著暮色四起，越發像是銀河的繁星。無論似在天上仙境或是在廣袤的景致中，都讓我全然沉醉，沉醉在孕

育中仲夏的美夢。

世界已沒有喧嚷和騷動，只剩下琴聲和風嘯蟲鳴。

如果可以，就讓風兒把它唱出來。來自遠方的花朵們，也跟著歡呼舞動。讓我可以穿透時間的空隙吧！看到夏夜那顆最燦明的星子。

我的繆斯將翩然而來，不再沉默。

因為當夕陽寂寞地沉落，當山谷的歌聲再度從我耳邊輕輕飄過。假如我是一隻鳥，我旋舞，我入迷地聽著。

我的心盼到了那開滿紅果子的樹，沿著林間溪谷。我歌唱，我雀躍。啊，睡去的山巒多寧靜。而我枕著一本詩集，望著窗外銀亮的月光，寫不盡的是至美山色。

－2018/07/30

－刊臺灣《臺灣時報》，2018/08/29，圖文。
－刊美國《亞特蘭大新聞》，2018/09/07，圖文。

18. 夏至清晨

哼著山歌的稻花上
坐著一隻介蟲殼兒，戲水
飛空一影子拖曳著影子
四面屏風
從跟前遛過

我擺脫了山后陰影
像綠光裡的羊
把腳步放慢
一條彎路連接無盡
水裡的雲追趕著月亮

18.　*Summer in the Morning*

Humming a folk song on the Rice flower
A cyprid sitting, playing the water
Gliding through the sky-----
shadow dragging the shadow
Wind blowing around
Passing through from me

I get rid of the shadow behind the mountain
Like a sheep in the green light
To slow down my steps
A crooked road leads to the eternity
Clouds chase the moon in water

—中英刊美國《亞特蘭大新聞》，
2018/07/27，山東大學外國語系吳鈞
教授 prof. Wu Jun 譯。

19. 夕陽，驀地沉落了

夕陽，驀地沉落了
在魚鱗瓦上
在老厝的茶園旁
一片灰雲
躲入我衫袖

時常跟著我
一步步奔躍向前的
小河
加快了步子
臨近新丘

就這樣
從河而來
翻飛的記憶

恰似風鈴花開
雖然披紅那堪早落

19. The setting sun , suddenly sank down

The setting sun, suddenly sinks down
On the scale tiles
By the old teahouse
A gray cloud
hides in my sleeves

Always follows me
<u>Jump</u> s and moves forward
The brook
Quickens his steps
Aproachhing the new hillock

Thus
Coming from the river
With the waving memories
Like the blooms of campanulas
Though still wrapped in red
But can't stand the early decline

　　　　—美國（亞特蘭大新聞），2018/07/27，吳鈞教授譯。

20. 漁　唱

那片金黃中有嫋嫋的歌聲。
浪似白梅有風提燈而過⋯⋯
小小的島攜著不可分割的斜灣
直到彼岸，那樣地琮綠，與柔和
透射著溫情的目光—
而守夜的我面對
黑沉沉的星空，
像幸福的歸帆，鐘聲一樣激盪⋯⋯

林明理 / 作畫

20.　*Song of　Fishing*

In the golden yellow there's singing curing up
Waves like white plum blossoms
Wind carries the lamp and passed by
A small island holds its tilted indivisible bay
To the other shore, such a jade green, and gentle
Through the warm eyesight─
Yet I ,the guard of the night facing
The deep starry sky
Like happy sails returning,
Like surging bells echoing ……

─中英詩畫刊美國《亞特蘭大新聞》，2018/07/27，山東大學外國語系吳鈞教授 prof. Wu Jun 譯。

21.玉山，我的母親

我沿著僻靜的石子路漫走

與你進行零距離親昵

即使大地沉睡如嬰

心中的力量讓我奮勇邁往—

一切妄念拋下

啊，金色的原野，坦露的胸膛

似母親溫柔深過海洋

多想將你緊貼我心，恒久激盪

21. Yushan Mountain, My Mother

I walk along the quiet gravel road
Close to you from zero distance
Even if the earth sleeps like a baby
The power of the heart gives me the courage---
I throw all of my improper thoughts
Ah, golden fields, bared chest
Like Mother's gentleness of the sea
How I want to bring you close to my heart
For lasting emotional dash

－中英刊美國《亞特蘭大新聞》Atlanta
Chinese News，2018.07.13，吳鈞教授
Wu Jun 英譯。

22. 憶　夢

哪裡去尋找
一種聲音
像枝葉間接力的蟬
在廣場前
新穀還有漸次消失的
田，老農撩起褲管
種菜插秧

啊小小的火窗
燃燒著希望
在溝岸旁
抓魚、游泳、釣蛙
油菜花和小雲雀嬉遊
街燈黯淡而溫暖

現在我知道
無論什麼季節
有一種聲音
像隻蟹，眼裡還沾著細沙
就迫不及待往岸上爬
它牽引著我，在清蔭的夜晚

註：火窗又稱迷你烘爐〈火爐〉，
　　在寒冬給老人家取暖用的。

22.　Recalling of the Dream

Where to look for
A voice
Like a relay of cicadas among the leaves
In front of the square
New grain and the gradually disappearing
Fields, the old farmer lifted his trouser legs
Growing vegetables and planting seedlings
Ah, the little fire window
With the burning hope
By the ditch
Fishing, swimming and catching frogs
Cole flowers and little larks are playing
Street lights dim and warm
Now I know
No matter what season it is
There is a voice
Like a crab , with silver sand stained on its eyes
Climb to the bank impatiently
It draughts me, in a cool and shading night

－中英刊美國《亞特蘭大新聞》Atlanta Chinese News，
2018.07.13，吳鈞教授 Wu Jun 英譯，水彩畫 1 幅。

23. 早 霧

窗臺外，遠處木犁
空蕩蕩地
單掛在田壟
那兒，山烟之上
你瞅著我，有好一陣
接著，我倚上沙發閉上眼睛
有如羊在霧中
想起了那年
瑟縮的二月
——透一股清冷

那是多久前的事兒了
我懷疑地問：
夜裏吹亂我頭髮的風
從上面經過 回聲
落滿了河谷
過去的日子彷彿
一切都很重要
又都不很重要
就像早霧頑皮地溜走
說了等於沒說

23. Morning Fog

Outside the window, the wooden plow beyond
Deserted
Hanging on the ribbing
There, upon the smoke of the mountain
you look at me, for rather a long time
Then, leaning on the sofa I close my eyes
as if a sheep in the fog
I remember that year
Curl up with cold in February
-------go through a kind of pure cold

That was something long time ago
I asked doubtfully:
The night wind blew and confused my hair
From above , echoing
Scattering upon the valley
The past days seemed
Everything is important
And also not very important.
Just like the morning fog gliding
What has said is like nothing has said

－中英刊美國《亞特蘭大新聞》**Atlanta Chinese News，2018.07.13**，吳鈞教授 Wu Jun 英譯。

24. 山居歲月

一聲磬中洗騷魂，
幾點霧雨迢曉月；
杏林徑裡有孤竹，
晚課聲中看鳥飛。

林明理 / 作畫

24. *Days in the Mountains*

With the sound of chime stone I came into meditation.

In the mist and drizzle I watched the moon afar

A lonely bamboo stands in the apricot grove

With evensongs my heart follows the flying birds.

－中英刊美國《亞特蘭大新聞》，2018/07/20，油畫 1 幅，山東大學外語系吳鈞 Wu Jun 教授譯。

25. 拂曉時刻

我們遇到迷霧
雖說還是冬季
湖塘微吐水氣
睫毛上也沾著露珠

細談中
一隻鷺在鏡頭前踟躕
這濕地森林
悄然褪色
萬物彷彿都在睡中

哪裡是野生天堂
如何飛離憂悒的白晝
我們啞然以對
只有小河隨心所願貌似輕鬆

25.　At Daybreak

We meet with dense fog
Although it's winter still
The pond gently spits up vapor
Dewdrops hang on our eyelashes

Chatting in detail
An egret is wavering before the camera lens
The wetland and forest
Fading away quietly
Everything seems to be in sleep

Where is paradise for the wild
How to fly away from the sorrowful daylight
We are mute for the answer
Only the brook seems to take it easy
Bubbling away willingly

－中英刊美國《亞特蘭大新聞》，
2018/07/20，油畫 1 幅，山東大學
外語系吳鈞 Wu Jun 教授譯。

26. 雨，落在愛河的冬夜

雨，落在愛河的冬夜
數艘白色小船上
在這多雨的港都，彩燈覆蔭下
獨自發送著溫顏

剎時，母親之河
廣大而平實
在那兒牽著勞動者的手
像從前，端視著我

啊，雨，落在愛河的冬夜
一隻夜鷺低微地呻吟
在這昏黃的岸畔，群山靜聆中
何處安置我僅存的夢？

哭吧，我以感動之淚
接受雨，和恩典
聽吧，時間的小馬上
我是永恆的騎士，覓尋黎明的歌者
是的，收起遊蕩的翅膀
那生命的薔薇早已關上了門
不再憂鬱地望著我，只有躲在冷黑中的風
任遊子潤濕了瞳孔

26. *Rain Falls in Love River at Winter Night*

Rain, falls in Love River at winter night
On a few small white boats
In the rainy reason on the port
Under the shade of colorful lights
Sending out the beaming warm

Suddenly, the mother river
Broad , simple and natural
Hand in hand with the laborers
In the usual way
Gazing at me

Ah, the rain, falls on LoveRiver in winter night
A night egret was moaning in the sky
On the dusky bank, mountains are listening
Where can I place my only dream

Crying, with my touched tears
I accept the rain, and the grace
Listen, the pony of time
I am the eternal knight,the singer of dawn

Yes, draw in my vagrant wings
The rose of life has long closed her door
She no longer gazes at me, only the wind
Hidden in the black cold
Allowing the wanderer wet their pupils

－中英刊美國《亞特蘭大新聞》，2018/07/20，油畫 1 幅，山東大學外語系吳鈞 Wu Jun 教授譯。

27. 書寫王功漁港

風車在漁港中歌唱
　漁港也在潮間中激響
望海寮上
一艘艘竹筏搖擺
　如整齊一致的黑武士

我踏著一抹斜陽
　經過圓拱橋和濕地
這兒水鳥飄忽，自由馳騁
　忽高忽低──
紅樹林説話
　招潮蟹説話
　　彈塗魚説話
像春風般清新
而我，是靜默的島

從夏夜翩翩而來
　佇在燈塔最高的視界

林明理／油畫作品

你所給我的
粼粼波光照影，曾是驚鴻
是盤旋不去的憶夢

註.王功漁港是彰化縣八景之
　一，位於芳苑鄉王功村西濱
　沿海，瀕臨台灣海峽，居民
　多以近海捕魚及沿海養殖
　為主。漁港裡黑白條紋的芳
　苑燈塔是台灣本島最高的
　燈塔，還有十座風力發電機
　組、造型獨特的圓拱橋、望
　海寮、濕地生態、竹筏、及
　夕照等景色。 -2018/08/03
─刊美國《亞特蘭大新聞》，
　2018/08/10，圖文。
─刊臺灣《臺灣時報》，台灣
　文學版，2018/10/19，油畫
　1幅。

28. 最美的時刻

有人說
某些時刻會永存不滅
那就是愛
那就是最美的時刻

我聽到
海波輕柔地撫慰著
夜已深沉
星叢紛紛匯聚而來

沒有人能阻攔你們
以歌接近天宇蒼穹
沒有人能如此樸實
以歌激盪這島嶼的幸福

是什麼
能唱出我們的苦痛和沉默

是什麼
能揭示昔日的回憶和歡樂

四十年過去了
你們仍以熱望擁抱未來
就像燃燒青春的火焰
共譜生命的讚歌

* 2018 年 8 月 6 日在電視上看到一部影片（四十年），
播出校園民歌盛行時期的歌手、作曲家的身影及其
音樂演唱會的實況記錄，令我內心澎湃不已，因而
為詩；在此特別感謝臺灣著名的音樂家胡德夫、李
宗盛及數十位歌手的熱情演出。

－2018/08/06

－刊美國《亞特蘭大新聞》，2018/08/17。
－刊臺灣時報，2018/09/12，圖文。

29. 想妳，在墾丁

每年落山風吹起
是墾丁旅遊的淡季
但我總會想起妳
如同孤鳥
整夜不眠地徘徊在
月光覆蓋的礁岩上

當我拾起貝殼，貼進耳裡
我就感到驚奇，彷彿

林明理油畫

那座軍艦石潛過大海
瞧，妳長髮如樹冠的葉片般
柔美而飄逸
瞬間，如夏雨

蘇鐵睡眠著、白野花兒睡眠著
甚至連星兒也那樣熟睡了
只有沉默的島嶼對我們說話 ——
就讓時間蒼老吧
這世界已有太多東西逝去
我只想擁有自然、夜，和珍貴的友誼

29.　*I Miss You, at Kending*

Every year when the northern-east wind blowing
It is the slack for traveling in Kending
But I shall alsway remember you
Like a lonely bird
The whole sleepless night lingering
On the moonlight covered reefs

When I pick up one shell, put it to my ears
I would always feel the wonder, as if
That rock of warship shaped moving in the sea
See, your long hair like leaves of crown of a tree
Gentle, beautiful and elegant
In a blink, like raining in summer
Cycad trees are asleep, white wild flowers are asleep
Even the stars are also sound asleep
Only the silent island talks to us----
Let the time getting old
Too many things in the world disappear
I only want to hold the nature, the night, and
The valuable friendship

（由山東大學吳鈞教授譯）
－中英詩刊美國《亞特蘭大新聞》，2018/08/10.

固定住，既能通風，也能防盜，我們孩子

偷食花生最終還是露了餡，被當場

贓的。

林明理博士詩畫

林明理油畫

想妳，在墾丁

每年落山風吹起
是墾丁旅遊的淡季
但我總會想起妳
如同孤鳥
整夜不眠地徘徊在
月光覆蓋的礁岩上

當我拾起貝殼，貼進耳裡
我就感到驚奇，彷彿
那座軍艦石潛過大海
瞧，妳長髮如樹冠的葉片般
柔美而飄逸
瞬間，如夏雨

蘇鐵睡眠著、白野花兒睡眠著
甚至連星兒也那樣熟睡了
只有沉默的島嶼對我們說話－
就讓時間蒼老吧
這世界已有太多東西逝去
我只想擁有自然、夜，和珍貴的友誼

I Miss You, at Kending

Every year when the northern-east wind blowing
It is the slack for traveling in Kending
But I shall alsway remember you
Like a lonely bird
The whole sleepless night lingering
On the moonlight covered reefs

When I pick up one shell, put it to my ears
I would always feel the wonder, as if
That rock of warship shaped moving in the sea
See, your long hair like leaves of crown of a tree
Gentle, beautiful and elegant
In a blink, like raining in summer
Cycad trees are asleep, white wild flowers are asleep
Even the stars are also sound asleep
Only the silent island talks to us----
Let the time getting old
Too many things in the world disappear
I only want to hold the nature, the night, and
The valuable friendship

恬靜

濱海公園旁海灣滄滄，
漁舟猶有奮力駛去的波紋，
我迷惑地望著遠方，
竟如此幸福，恬靜而溫暖！
瞧那橄欖青的、迷濛的
藍，還有浪花乍現－隨之喝采
特別是泊在岸沿的
雀鳥像神仙般
－接力地迴響，用喜悅替後山上彩。

2. Serenity

Drifting water of the bay by the Binhai park
Repples of fishing boats shooting out
With puzzles I look afar
Unexpectedly feel so happy, quiet and warm
See that olive- coloured , misty
Blue, the flowers of waves present, -
Following the cheers
Especially what berthed by the shore
The birds like angels
-relaying for the echoing
Adding colour of joy to the back mountain
（以上兩首詩由山東大學吳鈞教授譯）

書寫王功漁港

風車在漁港中歌唱
　漁港也在潮間中旋響
望海寮上
一艘艘竹筏搖擺
　如整齊一致的黑武士

我踏著一抹斜陽
　經過圓拱橋和濕地
這兒水鳥飄忽，自由馳騁
　忽高忽低——
紅樹林說話
　招潮蟹說話
　　彈塗魚說話
像春風般清新
而我，是靜默的島

從夏夜翩翩而來
　佇在燈塔最高的視界
你所給我的
粼粼波光照影，曾是驚鴻
　是盤旋不去的憶夢

註.王功漁港是彰化縣八景之一，位於芳苑鄉王功村西濱沿海，瀕臨台灣海峽，居民多以近海捕魚及沿海養殖為主。漁港裡黑白條紋的芳苑燈塔是台灣本島最高的燈塔，還有十座風力發電機組、造型獨特的圓拱橋、望海寮、濕地生態、竹筏、及夕照等景色。－2018/08/03

www. AtlantaChineseNews.com P.O. Box 941070 Atlanta, GA 31141-0070 Tel:770-455-0880 Fax:7

2018.8.10. Ming-Li

30. 晚　秋

夜霧瀰漫小山城
　河流在我眼底喧響
風依舊蕭索
　送來一地的寒
那叢綠中的野薑花
彷彿來自星群
從平林橋下的公園
飛出無數白蝶
　飛向水田
飛向和悅清澈的鏡面
忽地，一隻孤鷺
　　飛進我的愁緒
而明天
　陽光仍在花間跳舞
這鄉景的光華
　寂靜，如秋

林明理/作畫

　—刊臺灣《臺灣時報》，2018/10/10，圖文。
　—刊美國《亞特蘭大新聞》，2018/10/12，圖文，
　　圖是另一張油畫。

31. 恬 靜

濱海公園旁海灣澹澹，
漁舟猶有奮力駛去的波紋，
我迷惑地望著遠方，
竟如此幸福，恬靜而溫暖！
瞧那橄欖青的、迷濛的
藍，還有浪花乍現 —— 隨之喝采
特別是泊在岸沿的
雀鳥像神仙般
 —— 接力地喧響，用喜悅替後山上彩。

31 . Serenity

Drifting water of the bay by the Binhai park
Repples of fishing boats shooting out
With puzzles I look afar
Unexpectedly feel so happy, quiet and warm
See that olive- coloured , misty
Blue, the flowers of waves present, ——
Following the cheers
Especially what berthed by the shore
The birds like angels
—— relaying for the echoing
Adding colour of joy to the back mountain

（由山東大學吳鈞教授譯）

－中英詩刊美國《亞特蘭大新聞》，2018/08/10，吳鈞譯。.

32. 冬日神山部落

冬日大武山的寧靜裡
有神秘清昂的魔力：
柔和的光澤與雀榕樹的斑斕，
院牆小貓慵懶的哈欠聲；
霧嫋嫋的岩板巷，
環繞部落孤遺的地…

有時一隻五色鳥飛起，
宛若預告幸福的閃現，
又像是萬物靜止的終點。
我在魯凱族孩童身上
找回生命中不悔的歡愉。

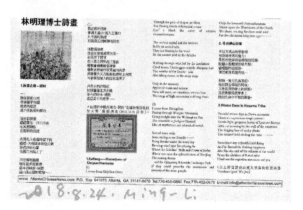

32.　*Winter Days in Koyama Tribe*

Peaceful winter days in Dawu mountain
There is a mysterious magic power :
Gentle light, gorgeous leaves of Sparrow Banyan
Little cat yawning by the wall of the courtyard
The fogging lane of rocky planks
The isolated field circling the tribe-----

Sometimes one colourful bird flying
As if to foretell the flashing happiness
Also like the end of the stillness of the world
From the children of Rukai tribe
I find out the regretless merriness and joy

山東大學吳鈞教授英譯　Translator：
Prof. Wu Jun

－中英詩刊美國《亞特蘭大新聞》，
2018/08/24，吳鈞譯。.

33. 秋在白沙屯

一根根巨大的
白色風車轉啊轉，
秋天的大海更加湛藍，
這是風和沙的故鄉，
山丘一片綠意。
我怎能錯過
相遇的悸動？
店仔街古厝的溫情，
多年不曾變樣，

金色的浪花翻滾跳躍，
陣陣秋風捲起潮浪，

林明理/油畫

年復一年的世代兒女
守望著這最後的古老。
啊讓我再一次發現——
那不可錯過的落日，
彷若天地間
只剩下我
和獨自吟唱的風。

*白沙屯位於苗栗縣
通霄鎮，是指白沙堆
積如山丘的意思。

－2018.8.29

－刊《笠詩刊》，第 327 期，2018/10，頁 85。
－刊《臺灣時報》，2018/10/03，圖文。
－刊美國《亞特蘭大新聞》，2018/10/12，圖文。

33. *Autumn in Baishatun*

*Dr. Lin Ming-Li

a huge root
The white windmill turns and turns.
The autumn sea is more blue,
This is the hometown of the wind and sand.
The hills are green.
How can I miss it?
The incitement of encounter?
The warmth of the old shop in the street,
Never changed for many years,

The golden waves roll and jump,
The autumn winds rolled up the tide,
Generations of children year after year
Watching this last old age.
Ah let me find it again--
The sunset that cannot be missed,
Like the heavens and the earth
Only me left
And the wind that sings alone.

　　　*Baishatun, located in Tongxiao Township, Miaoli County, means that white sand is piled up like a hill.
（Translator：天津師範大學張智中教授）

34. 秋日田野的搖曳裡

秋日田野的搖曳裡
溪牛蹣跚，蘆花飛揚
走在寧靜中
陽光淺淺鑴在海面上
不羈的大海啊，誰能
讀懂你的狂放？誰能
萌動你的心房？
我已走過數十個風霜
從不曾如此平靜
聆聽著大地聲響
就像你沉默地感受那樣
福爾摩沙的岩岸和沙岸
禾苗也綠得閃閃發亮
啊
最洶湧的波浪
從北極到南極
最龐大的海底山脈或
平原　丘陵和高山

林明理/作畫

如果我們用心聆聽
如果我們貼近大地
風依舊常新
蟲正鳴
島嶼也會歌唱

－刊臺灣《人間福報》，2018/10/04，圖文。
－刊臺灣《文學台灣》，第109期，2019年1月。
－刊美國（亞特蘭大新聞）圖文，2018/10/19。

35. 秋日的港灣

流動的時光羅織著晚浪
與幽微的漁火。
一片無人注意的蚵棚，
在鹹澀的雨中。

蘆花迴蕩的挽歌
被秋風輕輕挾起，移步向前。
古堡則把我的眼波下錨
繫住所有的懷念。

35.　*Harbor In autumn days*

Floating time nets the evening tides
And the dim lights on fishing boats
A reach of un-noticed shed of oyster
Soaked in the salty and astringent rain

Reverberating the elegies of the reeds
Raised up by the autumn wind gently ,and pushed
forward
The old castle anchorages the waves of my eyes
Holding all of my yearns and memories

（山東大學吳鈞教授譯）

　－中英譯刊美國《亞特蘭大新聞》，2018/09/28，吳鈞譯。

36. 給月芳

妳的友誼
多麼親切珍貴！
在溪水平靜的月色中，
彷彿乘著雲朵
從遠方疾馳而來——
抵達我的家園，
喚起我的思念與喜悅。

* 2018/07/24 收到《亞特蘭大新聞》許月芳
主編寄來刊登我的作品（民視「飛閱文
學地景」節目錄影紀實）的報紙，特此
致意。-寫於台東，2018/07/27。

－刊美國《亞特蘭大新聞》，2018/08/03。

37. 我的朋友

── 祝賀亞城許月芳主編

妳是和風，溫暖的手
　　環繞亞城每一角落；
而此刻妳的懷裡
存有一棵生命之樹，
　　庇護著亞城社區，
幫幫那些需要幫助者。
因為真情付出，才值得驕傲。
妳是愛的傳播使者，
　　無人知其背後的辛勞。

中間獲獎者為亞特蘭大新聞主編許月芳 (Atlanta Chinese News, Amy Sheu,) 和 CPACS CEO/ President Chaiwon Kim, （左），Vice President Victoria Huynh （右）。

　　註. 許月芳社長於 2018 年 9 月 24 日，榮獲泛亞社區服務中心（CPACS）頒發獎牌，特此祝賀。泛亞社區服務中心已成立 38 年，它是美國亞特蘭大私營非營利組織，任務是通過全面的健康和社會服務以及能力建設與宣傳來促進移民、難民等弱勢群體的獨立性和權益。

　　－2018.10.18 寫於台東。

http://www.atlantachinesenews.com/News/2018/09/09-28/B_ATL_P01.pdf

　　－刊美國《亞特蘭大新聞》，2018/10/19，照片 1 張。
　　－刊臺灣《金門日報》副刊，2018.11.02，照片。

38. 在後山迴盪的禱告聲中

雲影遮避了垂懸山緣的落日，
仍滴血的受難者
與罹難的親屬圍在夜裡…
…煎熬地等待，哭泣著。
大海，大海你啊！繼續
波濤洶湧。

攝影者：林明理

啊，我親愛的師長和罹難的學童
正緩慢地走上回鄉的路途。
願神拯救你們的靈魂
免於過多的痛苦和折磨。
願你們有祖靈的光
引領前行之路。
願你在安詳的國度裡
能跟隨天使的翅羽
步步升高……
而我的歌，
全島所有人合十的手，
在後山迴盪的禱告聲中，唉！

一滴淚輕微地　輕微地
在眼角中閃動。

　　*2018 年 10 月 21 日臺鐵普悠瑪發生意外事件，造成重大傷亡；僅以此詩為所有受難者及卑南國中罹難的師生哀悼。-2018.10.22

　　—刊美國《亞特蘭大新聞》，2018.10.26，圖文。

39. *Stay with my heart*

我聽到了你的聲音
啊，只是低低地傾訴
love you so much
that it is impossible to measure，
好似一場四季協奏曲
迴盪在黎明破曉時。

惱人的秋雨消失了，
迷霧散去的隱隱小路，
在我心中閃動著
那相遇而相知的片刻，
像命運般
　　　　向我席捲而來。

從陸海交界處飄來的雲
　　　撥開陰霾；
我的眼睛落在星星相連的
天空，而你始終沒有回來，
像是永恆的浪花反覆地說，
　　Stay with my heart.

　　　　－2018/9/14
　　　　－刊美國《亞特蘭大新聞》，2018/09/21

40. 獻給民視「飛閱文學地景」首播感言

那吉他聲
　音弦如此悠然
飄漾在淡水河裡，
紅毛城的影像在
　鏡頭中逐步靠近，
而我自己卻目不暇給地
　在時空中慢移。

感謝你們，讓淡水之夜
　美得輝耀，
兀立的老城多風采！
初冬的暖意
　染遍了漁舟水月，
橋畔以及所有一切
全都那麼美麗而炫目。

　　　　　　-2018.11.05 寫於台東

　*照片　1.詩人作家林明理，導演涂文權，執行製作石宛蓉合影於台北市「齊東詩舍」錄影後合照。

　*照片 2-3. 2018 年 11 月 3 日下午 4 點 55 分民視新聞「飛閱文學地景」首播作家林明理吟詩「淡水紅毛城之歌」，此作收錄於林明理雙語詩集《諦聽 Listen》，節錄文曾刊登在美國《亞特蘭大新聞》2018 年 8 月 29 日，特此向民視（FTV）製作組和亞城許月芳社長兼主編一併致謝。

　　－刊美國（亞特蘭大新聞），2018/11/09，圖文。

2018.11.09 Ming-Li

41. 悼

願諸神保護你…
…我親愛的鄉親和受難者，
因為正經歷垂死的邊緣和苦痛。
願神拯救你的靈魂於危險之中，
　從現在到沒有折磨。
願受難者親屬、甚至全島人民
　都一起來集氣，
讓失去生命的人
　有神的光引領他們前行之路。
讓存活者能腰身挺直，
　繼續將夢想完成。
而我只有在後山迴盪的禱告聲中，
　為你們虔誠禱告。感謝我的主。

攝影：林明理

　　　　* 追悼 2018 年 10 月 21 日臺鐵普悠瑪
　　　　發生意外事件。　　　-2018.10.26

　　　　　　－刊美國（亞特蘭大新聞）圖文，
　　　　　　2018 /11/02

42. 讀莫云《時間的迷霧 mist of time》

親愛的，妳的歌
恰似曙光下的一朵蓮，——
在兩山之間，在我心上。
儘管詩裡的每一行
有妳難以觸摸的內心的喜悅，
　　也有的是憂傷的...
　　　　陣陣共鳴的鄉愁。
在尋求著自由與安寧中，
妳永遠頌詠著光明，
是我純潔無瑕的朋友！

莫云著，台北秀威，
2018 年出版

　　*2018 年 12 月 17 日收到臺灣《海星詩刊》主編、台大中文系畢業的女作家莫云（本名宋淑芬）寄贈此書，細細讀過，倍感欣喜，因而寫詩祝賀。此書內容包含八十二首詩，詩的思想深邃，清雅、雋永。在後記裡，莫云寫道：「詩，是一種悸動，揮起覆蓋心靈的塵灰。」願她繼續寫出更多的現代詩來，我熱切地期望著。
--2018/12/18

　　　　－刊美國（亞特蘭大新聞），2018/12/21.
　　　　－刊臺灣（臺灣時報），2019/1/4

43. 讀李浩的新書有感

時代的巨輪不曾停歇...
在中國新征途上
　　又奮進了一百年，
我那麼近地閱讀你——
魯迅，一個中國新文學的先驅。
只要翻開歷史的記憶，以及
與你相關的若干人和事。
我深深以為：
你嚮往光明，光明也終於
打破黑暗，迎接 21 世紀白日。

著者：李浩
上海社會科學院出版
社，2018 年 9 月出版

　　*2018 年 12 月 5 日收到《上海魯迅研究》責任編委李浩遠
從上海寄來此書，感到欣悅。其著作包括《周文畫傳》、《許廣
平畫傳》等，主要從事魯迅相關文化研究。本書講究史料的考
察，使魯迅及其戰友之間深刻的聯繫更具歷史內涵，足以彰顯
魯迅對中國文學的思想價值與光采，這正是此書的成功之處。

　　－2018.12.5

43. On Reading Reading Li Hao's New Book

*Dr. Lin Ming-Li

The huge wheels of the era have never stopped its running ...
On the new journey of China
Another one hundred years of efforts have been made
I so closely read you —
Lu Xun, a pioneer in new Chinese literature
So long as the memory of history is opened, as well as
Some events and people which are relevant to you
My firm belief:
You yearn for light, which eventually
Breaks through darkness, to greet the 21st century

* On December 5, 2018, it was a joy for me to receive a book from Li Hao, an editor of *Research of Lu Xun in Shanghai*. Li Hao is mainly engaged in the research of Lu Xun, and his publications include *Pictorial Biography of Zhou Wen* and *Pictorial Biography of Xu Guangping*, etc. The book attaches importance to the examination of historical materials, which lends historical connotation to the relationship between Lu Xun and his comrades, hence to highlight Lu Xun's ideological value and importance in Chinese literature. Herein lies the success of the book.

December 5, 2018

（天津師範大學張智中教授英譯 Translated by Professor Zhang Zhizhong of Tianjin Normal University）

－刊美國（亞特蘭大新聞），2018/12/21。

44. 賴淑賢：《雪泥鴻爪異國情》

作為一個旅美學者，畢業於美國喬治亞大學教育博士的賴淑賢三十年來已為教育方面作出了貢獻，表現出奮發向上的精神和文學意趣的追求。她有顆高尚謙虛的心，關愛家人、朋友，也懸念師長及臺灣家鄉。《雪泥鴻爪異國情》是她的第一本散文著作，文中主題分為日本風情、美國風情、懷念故鄉和談天說地，大多敘述自己的所見所聞及看法。細讀其中，感受到了身為知識分子對學養與品格不懈的追求，也看到了她在學習過程的同時獲得了書香氣息的薰陶。

賴淑賢著，台北秀威，
2018 年出版

黑格爾曾說：「美就是理念的感性顯現」，而淑賢感性的文筆源於其真誠的內心。她以散文的文本，真誠坦率地流瀉細微的靈魂深處，表現其寬廣的文化視野，從而豐富自身的人文情思。作為一個作家，淑賢的文字裡優美的情趣，隨處可見。雖然，散文不講究聲律、辭藻，便於記事。此書抒寫了她一生中值得回憶的心情，用樸真之情描繪了故鄉的人、物、事及思念親人以排遣異國他鄉的孤寂。句句是對父母、恩師的一片深情，刻骨銘心，也飽含著求學及深沉的人生感慨和其孜孜以求的高尚人格。

全書包含七十三篇，它標誌著作者對文學和自身寫作有了新的提高，著重描寫其思念、異國情懷，並借助豐富的旅遊活動，生動地勾勒出一位博學多聞的作家形象。書前有政治大學傳播學院王前院長石番博士為序，還有作者自序。有幸獲贈此書，讓我能沉浸到她的世界中去感受其努力以赴、苦盡甘來的心路歷程及其身上閃射出奇麗的光彩。我期待著淑賢有更多的散文作品的不斷湧現。

－2018.11.30 寫於台東。

－刊美國（亞特蘭大新聞），2018/12/07。

45.南湖溪之歌

是自由的風不停地
　　帶著我
來到中央山脈的最深之處。
白雲躺在水裡，
　　花間野鳥妝點了高灘地。
小小山屋，在圈谷的邊緣...
南湖溪，你漾蕩的影子
　　在樹群和青草上晃動著。
沿溪而下，芒草林瑟瑟縮縮。
當風吹過
　　環山部落的吊橋，
我聽見了更高、更遠
　　更原始的山區，
有山椒魚和櫻花鉤吻鮭
　　在看不見的群峰裡的回聲。
我聽見了泰雅族耆老
　　在尋找兒時記憶的低語。
我聽見了水意和月光

油畫／林明理

向著碎石坡，循環往復。
我聽到了松林任由季節的更迭，
　　仍用深情的目光守望著...
　　　這一片野色如夢。
我聽到了海拔森林的呼喚，
　　那胡麻花的幻影，
　　那雲霧嬝繞的巨木步道，
　　那北國印象的天然雪景，
　　那屋宇層疊相間的山谷部落，
有我無盡的思念...在暮色中，
　　　　在時光之外。

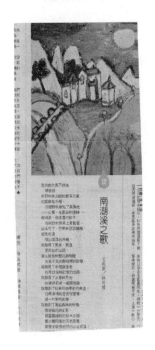

　　　　　　　　－2018.12.3

　　註：南湖溪是台灣高山河川，發源於南湖大山、南湖東山之間
圈谷，流域位於台中市和平區，溪長約三十公里，是大甲溪最遠源
流。南湖大山位於台灣太魯閣國家公園，屬台中市和平區，為中央
山脈第三高峰、在著名的台灣百岳之中，南湖大山與玉山、雪山、
秀姑巒山、北大武山合稱「五岳」，為台灣最具代表性的五座高山。
而保育的山椒魚已在地球存活了三億年，預計在未來十年，櫻花鉤
吻鮭也會在此當作放流鮭魚的路線，實值得我們高度的期待。

　　　　　　－刊臺灣，臺灣時報，2018/12/26，圖文。
　　　　　　－刊美國，亞特蘭大新聞，2018/12/21，圖文。
　　　　　　－刊臺灣《華文現代詩》Chinese modern poetry
　　　　　　　Quarterly，第 20 期，2019/02，頁 00。

45. 讀彭正雄編著:《圖說中國書籍演進小史》

在你熾熱的血液裡
有著鍾愛中國書籍的熱忱
　　和崇高的理想,
你輕輕擎起文化使命的火炬,
　　經風雨、歷歲月...
　　　　走過台灣一甲子。
從你那裡,我讀懂你歷經的滄桑,
　　　也為你感到驕傲。
　　你是本永不褪色的古書,
　　　　也是與眾不同的儒者。

　　*2018 年 12 月 22 日午後,收到出版家彭正雄(1939-)寄來贈書,甚為欣喜。近十年來,我在其出版社共出版過 13 本專著,每本書皆由他親自編製成書,因此對他感銘於心。《圖說中國書籍演進小史》是部探討中國歷代版刻的演變、古籍書版刻印刷版次的區別、古代書籍及其裝幀等內容的編著,並以圖說簡述,也可作為研究中國書籍演進的文史工作者或學生的參考書。彭先生從事出版事業已近一甲子,並於 2015 年 10 月 30 日受邀於台北淡江大學中文所博士班講授此書的相關內

容。他一生以文化出版人自居，其崇高形象及為海峽兩岸出版
業的辛勤付出，堪稱為台灣出版業的傑出代表，特此祝賀。

－2018.12.22

－刊美國（亞特蘭大新聞），2018.12.28

出版家彭正雄

附錄 appendix

1. 一隻勇敢飛翔的海燕

──讀梅爾的詩

一、其人其詩

　　走進梅爾（1968-）的深邃心靈，可以發現，她的最新詩集的編輯上更大氣、更雋永，更能凸顯獨特的性格內涵，因而彰顯《十二背後》這一部詩集的意義與價值。梅爾的詩題材與其行旅經歷、交遊生活是密切相關的。無論從布拉格到巴黎、莫斯科，或由丹麥到北京，巴西或秘魯…等世界各地，她記錄行程，描繪風景，並將之深深融合於自己的詩創作中。

　　如果說，浪漫的漂泊是梅爾生命的真相，那麼在她近幾年來的作品裡，其詩兼具地緣、宗教屬性，極大地拓寬了詩的題材領域，也激發了她最初的赤子之心，這是構成此部詩集的要素之一。而其本質特徵是意境深遠、語淡情濃的風格。抒情和咏物是其詩歌創作最重要的兩種類型，早在梅爾初期創作時期便已存在。但這三年多來，新的視覺正在改變其詩集文本。她以持之以恆的品行、橫溢的才華贏得了國際詩壇的尊重和賞識，成為世界詩人的一員，為江蘇詩歌推展的活動不遺餘力，也留下了許多令人稱讚的佳話，可謂是海峽兩岸交流的楷模。

二、梅爾詩歌的審美意蘊

通過梅爾的詩歌語言，在她的筆下，表現了有著深厚的文學藝術素養，對宗教與精神命題有深入的研究。她也在哲學、前世今生等領域，上下求索。我感受到的，她的詩歌帶給我們的多是有意味的、夾雜著詩人內心悲喜、複雜的情感和生命情懷。試看以下幾首詩句，她在詩（春之末）的第一小節裡寫道：

> 我離開你甚遠
> 荊棘的蠻荒之地寫滿寓言
> 冷卻之後，日子就像一粒粒鹽
> 從海水深處升起
> 我握著你的手
> 像握著那個世紀的憂傷

這首詩是梅爾的人生吟唱。詩人感嘆時間的流逝，在抒情中脫去了沉重，將人生感悟寄寓濃郁的情思。詩人敏銳地抓住了心理與複雜情感上的微妙變動，匯成了貫穿作品的主旋律，也將各小節的故事組結為一首詩歌整體，在落寞中喚起對往昔生活的親切感。近些年來，梅爾敞開的新視野，也解釋了其詩歌的藝術魅力。她對詩歌的想像書寫和思念鄉土的空間建構是雙線並行的。比如這一首令人動容的詩作（搖晃的森林）：

我帶著城堡、丹麥和一小塊石頭

開鑿大河，嫁給挪威

這洶湧的麥地，藍得

深過我的眼睛

波羅的海，犁開原始森林

讓我胸口的土地

變成琥珀的鄉愁

挪威，坐在一首歌裡

手捧一本書，會繼續飄過我

　　　　　　恍惚的

夢境

從上船的那一刻起，海盜

成為我的親人，所有的珍寶

鹹得讓人掉淚

　　此詩在細節確立的寧靜畫面中，意境及律動充滿了純真、感性。梅爾多思善悟，雖然常因事業而需跨越海域或乘坐飛機奔波往返。但因為詩歌是無邪的，也因為有它的存在，才能窺見梅爾的真性情。不管她飛翔得多遠多高，她的內心永遠有一種回歸自然純樸的理想。在她的詩歌中，隨著時間的推移和生活的變化，也善用擬人化的方式，形象地刻畫出她心中的想像和蛻變。如這首（夏天的蘋果）：

一只蘋果砸傷了我的翅膀

這個夏天　陽光明媚得耀眼

　　水總能濺起或大或小的水花
　　穿過湛藍的海洋　在另一邊
　　黑白顛倒地日夜輪迴

　　我並不能抓住時間的浮雲
　　就像我從來抓不住那些苦痛
　　帽子為我遮擋了雨水
　　可是層層阡陌　卻似故鄉的日頭
　　即便隔著再鹹的海水
　　一樣熱切而無奈

　　此時的詩人意識到有著本真的詩性自我，在靈魂深處她願追隨繆斯，也永不放棄她潛藏的夢想。這部詩集敷上了特異的文化色彩，也因而有了另一種節奏。她描繪出許多異國風光、也用富於感情色彩的詩語，非常典型地表現出了她的獨特性和題材的多樣性。比如這首（錯覺）：

　　我可以靜靜地躺在夜裡
　　在夢裡愛你
　　像那些黑暗
　　那些孤獨
　　那些不能抵達的觸摸

　　然後　忘掉你
　　像忘掉那些酒盅
　　那些從未存在過的親吻
　　在夜裡　在夢裡

　　睡眠像一頭多變的豹子

　　僅僅用花紋

　　詮釋一切

　　此詩流露出濃烈的哲學思辨與對愛情的感悟。作為詩人，梅爾並不盲目地崇信愛情的魔法和焦慮。但在蒼茫世事中，一顆漂泊的心也渴望有依依惜別的叮嚀，而不只是登高望遠時的沉吟。再加之梅爾特殊的人生經驗，可以說是在心靈的撞擊與情感的激發下之作；這也鑄造了她勇於愛其所愛的人格，也反應出她的成熟與深邃。

三、結語：努力向前成為梅爾創作的重要動因

　　顯然，近幾年來，梅爾的出現已引起了詩壇的關注。總的來說，她就像是一隻漂亮的海燕，像個善良的精靈，──高高地在海面上飛翔。在蒼茫的海上，她總是滿懷希望，勇敢地飛，衝著太陽的方向…努力向前，這也是梅爾創作的重要動因。就如她這首（雙河溶洞）的最後一小節裡寫道：

　　我在你青花瓷般的手勢裡

　　讀懂了鄉愁

　　七億年的寂寞與雷霆

　　都是你前生的腳步

　　一粒卵，在嶙峋的壁上繁衍

　　石頭與水

成為被朝聖的
圖騰

　　此詩寫得大氣，是梅爾內心情志的豐富表現。彷彿中，我被眼前一座宏觀的地景所吸引，跟著詩人的腳步看到溶洞神奇的全貌。她內心隱祕的重任，只能以詩更為深廣的內容來分擔，也有著一種時空交織的繁複之美。里爾克（Rainer Maria Rilke（1875-1926））曾說：「愛情──最神聖的嚴肅，然而亦是所有遊戲當中最美麗的。」梅爾的詩裡，愛情也是其主題之一，有的是純潔的思念的畫面，有的亦能揮灑出畫面以外更多的想像連結。此外，梅爾也是位成功的實業家，但並未影響她在詩壇的聲譽日益上升。最後，我僅以此文表達了對梅爾這部大著名至實歸的衷心祝賀。

－2018/12/27 寫於台東。

梅爾著，十二背后，人民文學出版社，2018 年初版。

－刊美國（亞特蘭大新聞），2019/1/25。

－刊臺灣（秋水）詩刊，第 179 期，2019 年預稿。

2. 林明理得獎及著作等事項記錄

1.2011 年臺灣「國立高雄應用科技大學 詩歌類評審」校長聘書。

2.詩畫作品獲收入中國文聯 2015.01 出版「當代著名漢語詩人詩書畫檔案」一書，山西當代中國新詩研究所主編。

3.2015.1.2 受邀重慶市研究生科研創新專案重點項目「中國臺灣新詩生態調查及文體研究」，訪談內文刊於湖南文聯《創作與評論》2015.02。

4.《中國今世詩歌導讀》編委會、國際詩歌翻譯研討中心等主辦，獲《中國今世詩歌獎（2011-2012）指摘獎》第 7 名。

5.獲 2013 年中國文藝協會與安徽省淮安市淮陰區人民政府主辦，"漂母杯"兩岸「母愛主題」散文大賽第三等獎。2014"漂母杯"兩岸「母愛主題」散文大賽第三等獎、詩歌第二等獎。2015"漂母杯"兩岸「母愛主題」詩歌第二等獎。

6.新詩〈歌飛霍山茶鄉〉獲得安徽省「霍山黃茶」杯全國原創詩歌大賽組委會「榮譽獎」榮譽證書 。

7.參加中國河南省開封市文學藝術聯合會「全國詠菊詩歌創作大賽」，榮獲銀獎證書〈2012.12.18 公告〉，詩作〈詠菊之鄉—開封〉。

8."湘家蕩之戀"國際散文詩徵文獲榮譽獎，散文詩作品：〈寫給相湖的歌〉，嘉興市湘家蕩區域開發建設管理委員會、中外散文詩學會舉辦，2014.9.28 頒獎於湘家蕩。

9.獲當選中國北京「國際漢語詩歌協會」理事〈2013-2016〉。

10.獲當選中國第 15 屆「全國散文詩筆會」臺灣代表，甘肅舉辦「吉祥甘南」全國散文詩大賽，獲「提名獎」，2015.7.26 頒獎於甘南，詩作〈甘南，深情地呼喚我〉，詩作刊於《散文詩‧校園文學》甘南采風專號 **2015.12**（總第 **422** 期）及《格桑花》2015"吉祥甘南"全國散文詩筆會專號。

11.2015.08 中國‧星星「月河月老」杯（兩岸三地）愛情散文詩大賽獲「優秀獎」，詩作〈月河行〉。

12.北京新視野杯"我與自然"全國散文詩歌大賽獲獎於 2015.10 獲散文〈布農布落遊蹤〉及詩歌〈葛根塔拉草原之戀〉均「二等獎」。

13.河南省 2015 年 8 月首屆"中國詩河 鶴壁"全國詩歌大賽，獲「提名獎」，詩作〈寫給鶴壁的歌〉。

14.2015.9 中央廣播電臺、河南省中共鄭州市委宣傳部主辦"待月嵩山 2015 中秋詩會詩歌大賽"獲三等獎，新詩作品〈嵩山之夢〉，獲人民幣 1 千元獎金及獎狀。

15.2012 年 9 月 9 日人間衛視『知道』節目專訪林明理 1 小時，播出於第 110 集「以詩與畫追夢的心－林明理」。

http://www.bltv.tv/program/?f=content&sid=170&cid=6750

16. 雲林縣政府編印，主持人成功大學陳益源教授，《雲林縣青少年臺灣文學讀本》新詩卷，2016.04 出版，收錄林明理新詩六首，（九份黃昏）（行經木棧道）（淡水紅毛城）（雨，落在愛河的冬夜）（生命的樹葉）（越過這個秋季）於頁 215-225。

17.北京，2015 年全國詩書畫家創作年會，林明理新詩（夢見中國）獲「二等獎」，頒獎典禮在 2015.12.26 人民大會堂賓館舉行。

18.福建省邵武市，2015.12.15 公告，文體廣電新聞出版局主辦，邵武"張三豐杯海內外詩歌大賽"，林明理新詩〈邵武戀歌〉獲「優秀獎」。

19.安徽詩歌學會主辦，肥東縣文聯承辦，第二屆"曹植詩歌獎"華語

詩歌大賽，林明理獲二等獎，獎狀及獎金人民幣兩千，2016.3.28
中國煤炭新聞網公告。

http://www.cwestc.com/newshtml/2016-4-2/406808.shtml

http://www.myyoco.com/folder2288/folder2290/folder2292/2016/04/20
16-04-22706368.html 來源：肥東縣人民政府網站 發佈時間：
2016-04-22。詩作（〈寫給曹植之歌〉外一首）刊於中共肥東縣委
宣傳網 http://www.fdxcb.gov.cn/display.asp?id=37800

20.北京市寫作學會等主辦，2016 年"東方美"全國詩聯書畫大賽，新
　詩（頌長城），榮獲「金獎」。

21. 2016"源泉之歌"全國詩歌大賽，林明理新詩（寫給成都之歌）獲
　優秀獎，中國（華西都市報）2016.6.16 公告於
　http://www.kaixian.tv/gd/2016/0616/568532.html

22.2016.11.19 民視（FORMOSA TELEVISION）下午三點五十七分首
　播（飛閱文學地景）節目林明理吟誦（寫給蘭嶼之歌）。
　https://www.youtube.com/watch?v=F95ruijjXfE

https://v.qq.com/x/page/e0350zb01ay.html 騰訊視頻

http://www.atlantachinesenews.com/ 2016.12.2 美國（亞特蘭大新聞）
　刊民視【飛閱文學地景】林明理吟詩（寫給蘭嶼之歌）於首頁網，
　可點播

http://videolike.org/video/%E9%A3%9B%E9%96%B1%E6%96%87%E
5%AD%B8%E5%9C%B0%E6%99%AF 【飛閱文學地景】video
https://www.facebook.com/WenHuaBu/posts/1174239905989277

23.2016.12.24 民視晚上六點首播（飛閱文學地景）節目林明理吟誦
　（歌飛阿里山森林）。
　https://www.youtube.com/watch?v=3KAq4xKxEZM

http://www.woplay.net/watch?v=3KAq4xKxEZM

騰訊視頻 https://v.qq.com/x/page/s03601s7t0z.html
（飛閱文學地景）IVEP25

24.詩作（夏之吟），2015.1.2 應邀於《海星詩刊》舉辦【翰墨詩香】
活動於台北市長藝文中心聯展。

詩作（那年冬夜），2017.2.4 應邀於《海星詩刊》舉辦【詩的影像】
活動於台北市長藝文中心聯展。

http://cloud.culture.tw/frontsite/inquiry/eventInquiryAction.do?method=showEventDetail
&uid=586f3b1acc46d8fa6452ca16 臺灣的「文化部網」

25.義大利（國際閱讀委員會）（international Reading Committee）頒
獎狀給林明理於 2017.04.21.

26.2017.7.15 民視 FTV（Taiwan Formosa live news HD）晚上六點首
播（飛閱文學地景）節目林明理吟誦詩（白冷圳之戀）。

https://www.youtube.com/watch?v=6b17mmHQG3Q
http://videolike.org/view/yt=f2pgDDqzScz

27.林明理散文作品（寫給包公故里－肥東），獲 2017 年第三屆中國
包公散文獎徵文比賽 B 組散文詩三等獎，收編入中共安徽省肥東
縣委宣傳部，肥東縣文聯舉辦，第三屆"中國•包公散文獎"獲獎作
品集，【中國散文之鄉】。

28.林明理新詩《寫給麗水的歌》獲得浙江省麗水市"秀山麗水·詩
韻處州"地名詩歌大賽三等獎。2018 年 1 月 4 日下午 2 點在麗水
市麗水學院音樂廳參加麗水市"秀山麗水·詩韻處州"地名詩歌朗誦
暨頒獎儀式。麗水新聞網 http://www.lishui88.com/n36567.htm

29.2018.11.03 民視 FTV（Taiwan Formosa live news HD）下午 4 點 55
分首播（飛閱文學地景）節目林明理吟誦詩（淡水紅毛城之歌）。

https://www.youtube.com/watch?v=ky76TlKxe8M

3. 林明理專書 monograph

1.《秋收的黃昏》The evening of autumn。高雄市：春暉出版社，2008。

2.《夜櫻-林明理詩畫集》Cherry Blossoms at Night。高雄市：春暉出版社，2009。

作品賞析》The Imagery and Connetation of New Poetry-A Collection of Critical Poetry Analysis。臺北市：

合-當代詩文評論集》The Fusion Of Art and Nature。臺北市：文史哲出版社，2011。

5.《山楂樹》HAWTHORN Poems by Lin Mingli（林明理詩集）。臺北市：文史哲出版社，2011。

6.《回憶的沙漏》（中英對照譯詩集）Sandglass Of Memory。臺北市：秀威出版社，2012。

7.《湧動著一泓清泉—現代詩文評論》A GUSHING SPRING-A COLLECTION OF C O M M E N T S O N MODERN LITERARY WORKS。臺北市：文史哲出版社，2012。

8.《清雨塘》Clear Rain Pond（中英對照譯詩集）。臺北市：文史哲出版社，2012。

9.《用詩藝開拓美—林明理讀詩》DEVELOPING BEAUTY THOUGH THE ART OF POETRY – Lin Mingli On Poetry。臺北市：秀威出版社，2013。

10.《海頌—林明理詩文集》Hymn To the Ocean（poems and Essays）。臺北市：文史哲出版社，2013。

11.《林明理報刊評論 1990-2000》Published Commentaries1990-2000。

臺北市：文史哲出版社，2013。

12.《行走中的歌者─林明理談詩》The Walking singer-Ming-Li Lin On Poetry。臺北市：文史哲出版社，2013。

13.《山居歲月》Days in the Mountains（中英對照譯詩集）。臺北市：文史哲出版社，2015。

14.《夏之吟》Summer Songs（中英法譯詩集）。英譯：馬為義（筆名：非馬）（William Marr）。法譯：阿薩納斯 · 薩拉西（Athanase Vantchev de Thracy）。法國巴黎：索倫紮拉文化學院（The Cultural Institute of Solenzara），2015。

15.《默喚》Silent Call(中英法譯詩集)。英譯：諾頓 · 霍奇斯（Norton Hodges）。法譯：阿薩納斯 · 薩拉西（Athanase Vantchev de Thracy）。法國巴黎：索倫紮拉文化學院（The Cultural Institute of Solenzara），2016。

16.《林明理散文集》Lin Ming Li´s Collected essays。臺北市：文史哲出版社，2016。

17.《名家現代詩賞析》Appreciation of the work of Famous Modern Poets。臺北市：文史哲出版社，2016。

18.《我的歌　MY SONG》，Athanase Vantchev de Thracy 中法譯詩集。臺北市：文史哲　出版社，2017。

19.《諦聽　Listen》，中英對照詩集，Dr.William Marr 英譯，臺北市：文史哲出版社，2018。

20.《現代詩賞析》Appreciation of the work of Modern Poets，臺北市：文史哲出版社，2018。

21.《原野之聲》Voice of the Wilderness，臺北市：文史哲出版社，2019。